Inspirations
On the Path of Blame
Shaikh Badruddin

Inspirations
On the Path of Blame
Shaikh Badruddin of Simawna

An Interpretation and Commentary by
Shaikh Tosun Bayrak al-Jerrahi al-Halveti

THRESHOLD BOOKS
Putney & Brattleboro, Vermont

Threshold Books is committed to publishing books of spiritual significance with high literary quality. All Threshold books have sewn bindings and are printed on acid-free paper.

We will be happy to send you a catalogue.
Threshold Books, RD 4, Box 400, Putney, Vermont 05346

A publication of the Halveti-Jerrahi Library of Sufism
The Jerrahi Order of America
884 Chestnut Ridge Road,
Chestnut Ridge, New York 10977

Cover design courtesy of Shems Friedlander

Copyright © 1993, all rights reserved.
10 9 8 7 6 5 4 3 2 1

ISBN 0-939660-47-4

Library of Congress Cataloging-in Publication Data

Ibn Qadi Simawnah, Badr al-Din Mahmud, d. 1416?
 [Waridat. English]
 Inspirations on the path of blame / Shaikh Badruddin of Simawna ; a commentary by Tosun Bayrak Al-Jerrahi Al-Halveti.
  p. 160
  ISBN 0-939660-47-4 (alk. paper) : $13.00
  1. Sufism—Early works to 1800. I. Bayrak, Tosun. II. Title.
BP188.9.I2713 1993
297'.4—dc20   93-7556
                                                CIP

CONTENTS

THE OPENING by Kaygusuz Abdal 9

INTRODUCTION 30

    On Sufism 41
    On Malamiyyah 44
    The Malami's Attitude toward Evil and Hypocrisy 48
    The History of Malamiyyah 54

INSPIRATIONS 69

    Chapter I:
    The Divine Verse 70

    Chapter II:
    The Hereafter 77

    Chapter III:
    On the Limitations of Physical Existence 83

    Chapter IV:
    On the Revelation of the Mysteries to the Knowers of Allah 88

    Chapter V:
    The Nature of Reality 102

    Chapter VI:
    The Reality of Muhammad 114

    Chapter VII:
    The Mystics 128

    Chapter VIII:
    Manifestations of the Inner Self 134

    Chapter IX:
    The Human Being 137

    Chapter X:
    The Prophet Jesus Christ 147

Dedication

This book is dedicated to the blessed souls of Hajji Bayram Wali and Sayyid Muhammad Nur al-'Arabi. Most of this book is derived from their enlightened commentaries. May Allah Most High be pleased with them and praise their souls at the highest levels of His paradise, close to His throne and under that banner of Allah's glory, which is held by Allah's mercy upon the universe, our master Muhammad (Allah's peace and blessings upon him). And may their followers deserve their intercession in this world and in the Hereafter. —*Amin*

Bismillah ir-Rahman ir-Rahim

The text that follows is derived from the *Budala-name* (A Letter from One Who Gave Himself Up to Receive His Lord) of Kaygusuz Abdal (d. 1444/848 H). It can be found in Nuruosmaniye Library, Istanbul, Manuscript #4904.

* * *

In the Name of Allah, the Compassionate, the Merciful

The Opening

(A Letter from One Who Gave Himself Up to Receive His Lord)

Kaygusuz Abdal

In the beginning He is beyond the lowest and the highest, further than the front and behind the back, more to the right than right and more to the left than left.

He has no name or attribute at a place called Void, hidden in the matter of all words, where there is neither word, nor name, nor light, nor weight, nor form, nor place.

> Surely Allah is with Himself alone, without need of His creatures. (Qur'an: Ankabut, 29:6)

> Allah was, and nothing was with Him. (hadith)

> And with Him are the keys of the Unseen. None knows them but He. (Qur'an: An'am, 6:59)

> Surely there came upon man a time when he was nothing that could be told with words. (Qur'an: Insan, 76:1)

> Glory be to our Lord, the Lord of Might, above what one can describe. (Qur'an: Saffat, 37:180)

> He was a hidden treasure. . . . (hadith qudsi)

At that timeless time when there is no before or after, in that void where there is nothing evident or hidden, in eternity before the beginning and the end, was a pure He, the divine identity.

When He wished to be known, He said "Be."

He struck the sound of the first letter upon the sound of the second, and a single dot formed within the endless void. The dot moved down, became a line, like One [*Alif*, the letter A in Arabic]. And He picked up the end of the line and moved it upwards, a concave curve. He put a dot under it and made the letter *B*.

Well before all that happened, I was with Him.

Before I wore the clothes of Adam, I was alive within the being of the Divine unseen, until He wished to show Himself to Himself.

Then he moved the dot from right to left; some things He dotted, some not. He set the twenty-eight letters in Adam's face. He built the seven worlds below his waist, the seven heavens above, placed His footstool upon his chest and His throne upon his head, and taught him His Names. And with His Beautiful Names He showed Himself to Himself.

In the eighteen thousand universes that He set between the *B* and the *E*, He made His creatures two by two. Then He put a dot from a man's loins in a mother's belly and dressed it in Adam's clothes and His mercy—for He made me for Himself, and everything else for me.

Thus I came with Adam from Eden into the open, from the light of the dark into the darkness of sunlight.

When I saw my many selves I forgot the One. I wanted this and that, running hither and thither, gathering this and losing that, turning in circles; I knew not what I did. And oh! No one had pity on me.

One day, again, wearing my mother's clothes and riding my father's horse, I was running in circles. I heard a voice say, "Enough! Come back to me now!"

As if I had never before been or been able to see, I found myself all new, in the middle of an endless plain. I saw seventy-two nations looking for something, running each other down. I joined one, fought the other, then joined the other and made armistice. After receiving a thousand wounds and being healed a thousand times, I ran away to a lonely dune.

I saw a city far beyond. Alone I walked, day and night. Each day the city seemed further away.

One day, when my doubt was about to overrun my hope, a boy appeared from nowhere. He had a beauty hard to describe, as hard as describing the beauty of love. Light shone from him, leaving no shade or shadow around him. He saluted me, saying, "May you be blessed with love."

I said, "Indeed, nothing is ever reached without it."

"Why do you wander in this desert?" he asked.

"This seems to be the way to that city in the distance."

"If you really wish, I will take you there," he said. Then he put a collar around my neck, tied a rope to it, and pulled me behind him like a dog.

In no time I was in the city. I found myself all alone—no guide, no collar, no rope. I searched every corner of the city from one end to the other; no one was there. But all around me was everything I had ever desired, every gem, every precious thing. And I said to myself, "Aha! I am the one whom I know I am!"

A terrible fever seized me. I evaporated from matter into meaning and from meaning I turned back into flesh, over and over again.

Then all of a sudden I found myself in the midst of a crowd. One hundred and twenty-four thousand men of God were there—Muhammad (peace and blessings upon him), Allah's beloved; Jesus, fruit of His soul; Moses, with whom He talked; Abraham, His closest; and Adam, His choicest one—all were there, and His blessings upon them all.

They showed me a place and sat me amongst them. Then one said, "O seeker, if you know the tongue of the birds, then speak, tell us your truth. If not, keep your silence, or better, leave."

Woe to me, I thought, my tongue is the hunter, and I have fallen into its trap! Now either I speak and am saved, or I am lost forever. And I spoke.

"The heavens are the dome of this sacred school. The sun and the moon and all the planets are lamps so that I can distinguish my hope for wisdom and rid the darkness of my self. The earth is my flesh; the oceans and rivers are in my veins; the sky is my abode; and beyond is my pleasure ground. The time is mine, and the worlds whirl around me. The stars are the torches I point to places I wish to go.

"The nights are the secret of sanctity; the days are the clarity of prophecies. Birth is spring; death is fall; health is a rose garden; sickness a dungeon; lying, a rogue; truth, manhood; sleep, supplication; heedfulness, to know.

"Heart, at ease, is paradise; in constriction, hell. Intellect is Gabriel; learning is the value of life; money, weight.

"Misery to the miser; joy to the generous; darkness to the faithless; unity to the enlightened. Exhilarated be the lover; doomed, the ignorant; tormented, the misbehaving. Light in the heart of the just; fire to the tyrants; blessings upon the sage; power to the brave; security to the young.

"Sun descends; the waters rise. All is one and everlasting, and all is mine. I am the master and I am the slave. . . ."

They all cried: "Well said, dervish! What was it that you told—a story, a dream, or your imagination?"

"No!" said I, "It is God's truth, for no one belongs to other than Allah. This indeed is the state of the son of your brother. All this happened to me. He who tells of things he has not seen or been is not worthy to be called a man!"

And again one day I found myself in a desert, with no end in sight. Might it be the space of my imagination? But I kept on a road right through its center. Might it be the cycle of time?

So I kept on walking, with no end in sight, nor was there any

The Opening

other there beside me. Is it that all else had entered into me?

No, there must be others; there must be more than one! So I talked to myself:

> All is in Me; there is none other than I.
> I am the being that became when He said, "Be."
> I am the life and the only living.
> I am the love, the lover, and the beloved.
> In human shape is all and everything.
> In the shape of His mercy He made Me.

In that "I," I saw the Core where there is no time, nothing to relate nor compare. In this visible world is the invisible—the world of angels and the world of thought and the power of God and the heavens of essence where no idea resides, where there is no difference or likeness.

Is this a dream, an illusion? There is no one to ask.

I stopped to reflect. I stuck my head out from myself, and I saw the endless desert again. I pulled back my head and there was no road, no distance, no desert or space, nothing but "I."

I said to myself, "In all, I am the Truth. I am the truth of it all. There is no why or wherefore. In the ocean of Its cause even the Absolute is drowned. Mansur is not; Baghdad is not; and that which he said—'I am the truth!'—also is not!"

As I uttered these words an old man appeared—white-bearded, lips trembling in silent litany, fingering his long prayer beads, a long staff in his other hand, a big turban on his head, the cloak of shaikhs on his back—by all the signs, a wise man.

I approached him with great respect and greeted him, wishing Allah's peace and blessings upon him, hoping he would tell me the secret of this land.

He did not respond but kept muttering litanies and playing with his beads.

I said, "O venerable one, I gave you the salutations of God, why do you not respond?"

The old man cried, "Do you dare to interrupt my litanies with your salutations?" and lifted his staff to strike me.

I threw away my coat and took hold of a stick to defend myself . . . but seeing me fearless, the old man fled. I ran after him and grabbed him.

"Why do you run away? All I wanted was to ask you a question!"

"I ran away because I fear the brave!" he said. "Now you have caught me. Ask what you will."

"Who may you be?" I demanded. "And how did you appear in this desert? And where are we?"

He said, "I am on the earth and in the air and everywhere. Everybody everywhere usually obeys me, but you seem to be different.

"This place is the Desert of Woe. So many Solomons and Davids, kings and men of God, have sunk in its quicksand! Now you can't even find their signs.

"As to who I am, what does it matter? Many take me as their master."

"I must know who you are, for you came upon my way," I said. "Please tell me."

He said, "I was very well known to God, ambitious to please and praise Him. Many thousands of years I worshipped Him, seeking His pleasure. Only once did I do wrong, jealous of the one He chose above me—when I knew that I was much better than he! And alas, this one little vanity has given me such a bad name!"

Then I knew who he was—my own devil, Satan. I took refuge in Allah from him, and I took refuge in my soul from my flesh, and I ran away from him. . . .

I ran until I found a huge tree which appeared in the center of the desert. It had five limbs, much like a man's head and arms and legs. Its shade covered a vast, cool place from east to west. I lay under it and fell asleep.

The Opening

I dreamt. The tree turned into a face. One branch became eyes and saw, another became ears and heard. A third became a mouth to taste; a fourth, a nose to smell; a fifth became cheeks to feel touch. And the head was of the Prophet Muhammad, Allah's peace and blessings be upon him. And I saw a high throne at the foot of the tree, so large that all the prophets and saints had room to sit on it, and at the center was Muhammad (peace and blessings upon him). They all asked him one question: "How is it that the Turks call a large camel a camel, like everybody else, but they call a small camel a *köçek*? Is not a small camel a camel too?"

The Messenger of Allah said, "A camel is a camel whether small or large. The names may differ but the named is the same. In truth, all is one and the same."

I too asked a question of the Messenger of Allah. "What place is this, what tree is this?"

The Blessed One said, "This place is the Ka'bah of heaven and earth, where the two meet. It is the moment, the now. This tree is the Tree of Being, in the shape of Man. It has five limbs. Upon the two top branches the light falls. One of them is the mind; the other is my eyes, by which the truth is seen. Light reflected from these two branches touches one of the other three. That is the tongue of my followers who tell the truth. Upon the two lower branches no light falls; they are in the dark. They are the ears and the nostrils of the faithless and the ignorant: they neither hear the promises of the garden nor smell its perfume."

I pulled myself within, to reflect upon the meaning of this ... and when I looked up I was alone again. I said, "I am the moment. I am the only one." And this verse came out.

> I knew not I.
> Until the lover leaves,
> the Beloved is.
> When there is no flesh, no life,
> neither beast nor man is left.

Inspirations

> The drop is the ocean;
> the seen is the unseen.
> Then the unseen is seen.
> The slave is the sultan;
> the sultan is the slave.
> I am neither the sultan nor the slave,
> neither the lover nor the beloved,
> neither faithful nor without faith.
> Neither am I on the path; nor is there a path.
> Neither time nor space.
> Neither am I dust blown by the wind.
> Neither am I water to mix the clay.
> Neither heart nor mind nor soul.
> I am the secret of the secret.

I looked in all directions, and there was no one.

All that the heavens and the earth contained was now hidden in me. From every single thing a voice was echoing within me; yet I heard my voice say, "I was once on this earth and under this sky. Now all are inside. Wherever I look I see my face. Waters flow; the winds blow. The sun, the moon, the galaxies whirl within."

As I went deeper I entered the city of the mind. I saw the Beloved of Allah, Muhammad Mustafa (peace and blessings upon him)—and I realized. Below this I entered the city of love. I saw 'Ali al-Murtada (may Allah be pleased with him)—and I loved.

I said to him, "O my sultan, whose city is this, whose beautiful gardens, canopies, and palaces? I see no owners."

'Ali (may Allah be pleased with him) said, "Is there a place without an owner? Is there a being without a master? The owner of both worlds, material and spiritual: all is His and is from Him. He is the one that is seen, and He is the one who sees. Nothing is without Him, and all that exists is His."

I held the blessed hand of Hadrat 'Ali and begged him to take me as his slave, to teach me the foundation, without which nothing stands, and the order of things—one by one, to add up to one.

He took me, and I stayed with him a long time. One day I asked him, "Master, tell me: were we not with Him? Before we entered into this flesh, did we not mark out our fate together, with Him? And even when I saw myself within this flesh, I found myself upon His world and under His sky. Then one day I saw that what was outside—the flesh, the world, the heavens—was all in me. What is this mystery?"

When I said this, my master disappeared. Then I knew that he also had entered into me.

Sometime later I found myself in the court of Solomon. Men and jinn, birds and beasts, all were gathered around him. And that prophet was telling them their duties, according to their abilities. I caught him talking to the giants—wild, ignorant, part animal, and huge. He said to them, "Go wash with torrents of water and cleanse yourself of your faults which are as large as yourselves. Perchance you may be purified, or else God's wrath will be great."

I came closer to see the blessed face of Solomon, and lo, I saw my master 'Ali looking at me from Solomon's eyes. My heart and soul flowed unto him. Without words I begged him for an answer. Wordless he replied, "I am now Solomon, and Solomon does not know. He takes me for himself. I know what I am doing."

I waited a long time to find my master by himself, alone. One day so finding him, I asked, "Master, tell me the story of Joseph. How is it that he was thrown into the well?"

"O son, the deep dark well is this body of flesh and bone. When Joseph left the well, he became sultan of Egypt. He became the master of his true being when he left the desires of his flesh." Then 'Ali (may Allah be pleased with him) asked me to close my eyes, and I saw all the words in the Qur'an and the one hundred and twenty-four thousand prophets confirm and praise what my master had said.

Then I saw Muhammad, Allah's mercy upon the universe,

leading all the other prophets to the absolute truth that is Allah (His peace and blessings upon all of them). I mixed amongst them. When we reached the altar of truth, we stood at a respectful distance.

The Beloved of Allah came forward and stood close to Allah and said: "O my Lord, you are the owner and the master of this sinful lot. We are your servants. We have none to turn to but you. You made me the intercessor, the one who praises, and the one who is thankful for all, and these are all a part of me. By these who are my parts you made me know myself, and you made me whole. I beg you, have mercy. Forgive us all."

And the Lord spoke: "O my beloved, they may all be in you, as all my Beautiful Names are in you; yet each of them relates to me differently. It is by only one of my attributes that each of them knows me. And only I know them."

"Now look," said Allah Most High. And Muhammad (peace and blessings upon him) looked . . . and saw only Adam (upon him be peace), the father of everyone, the first man.

And I looked . . . and he was I. And no one else was there. And I said:

> Lo! I am made the sultan of the universe.
> I am the mine from which came the gem of life.
> I am the ocean of microcosm in each soul.
> All found their shape and form in me, in Man.

Sight within sight: I saw a whole other world, its creatures all asking each other, "What is this land, with all these cities, towers, and palaces? Who are the owners?" I was in their midst facing a throne. They asked me, "Whose throne is this?"

"Only the ones who have been here know," I told them. "I have come to this land thousands of times, and I saw it like this. There is someone called Adam who came here, and I came with him." As I was speaking, Adam came by. "That is he," I said.

They came to him and kissed his hand. "What is this land,

The Opening

and who is the owner of this throne?" they asked.

He replied, "Allah is my witness. I don't know any more than you do! I set foot here a moment before you, and I saw it as you see it."

At that moment I knew what to do. "O Lord, this secret is known to my heart." I prayed, "My heart is your mirror." And I knew.

Now Adam asked them a question. "Who is this man who claims he knows?"

"We found him here when we came."

He turned to me. "And who may you be?"

"I am the one who I know I am."

But Adam did not hear. "Tell me, please, who are you?"

"I have passed through this place, which is like an inn, thousands of times," I said. "Sometimes I am the only guest; sometimes I have neighbors. Mine is a long story. But how is it that you do not know your own son? I am he."

Adam said, "I know you not!"

I told him that I had been with him in Paradise, but he did not believe me. I told him what had happened to him in the garden when he ate the forbidden fruit—how he had descended from the best of the best to the worst of the worst—and that I had descended with him. I told him how many times he had brought me to earth, and how I became earth, and how he took me to himself, and I became human. . . .

No wonder he forgot me. His sons and daughters are so many.

Then I told him how the angel Gabriel had taught him to work the land, how our mother Eve gave birth to twenty children—each son she married to the daughter born after him. I told him how his firstborn son, Cain, wanted to have his firstborn daughter; how he had hated the second-born Abel and killed him; and how, because he cursed Abel, all his sons and daughters, and I amongst them, inherited pain.

I told him that all the messengers of Allah had suffered from his sin—Noah, too. For nine hundred years he called his people to truth, and they denied him. I told him how a son of Cain had thrown a rock at Noah and broken his head. Noah had cursed him, too—and Allah, pouring waters from heaven to cleanse the blood pouring from his blessed face, drowned those who denied him. I told him how Noah saved the ones who believed in him, in his ark, and how the rest died in the flood. (The flood still exists, and the unbeliever drowns in it, for those who do not know the truth keep drowning in their ignorance.)

Then I told him the story of the pain of Job, who had twelve sons, all exalted and beneficent—who remembered his Lord and worshipped incessantly. One time his enemy and mine, the accursed Devil, came to him in the shape of his shepherd and reported that all his herds, ten thousand in number, had died of cold; yet Job did not cease praying. The Devil returned as the keeper of his camels and told Job that all had drowned. Job took no notice. Back came the Devil as the foreman of Job's land, announcing that his harvest was ruined. He found no response. In the shape of a maid he came, crying that Job's palaces were destroyed by earthquake, his children and people dead. Still the heart of Job did not tighten; he did not forget. As Job prostrated in thankfulness, Satan entered him through his nose and opened gaping holes in his body; yet he could not touch that heart filled with the Lord nor that tongue filled with His names. Job just kept saying, "Praised be the Lord."

I told Adam the story of John the Baptist, the son of Zachariah, who was martyred inside the tree. I told him of the coming of Buht an-Nasr, who took their revenge on the king of the time, the king who murdered Zachariah and John the Baptist both. They killed seventy thousand children and supporters of the king, for they were the opposite of the opposite, and opposites are enemies to each other; they kill themselves by killing each other.

I told Adam the story of Joseph, the son of Jacob, and that

of Jesus and Moses, Allah's peace and blessings be upon them all. And Adam saw it all in himself, the evil in his flesh and the salvation in his soul.

Then I said, "O Adam, let us go within ourselves and watch how the accursed Nimrod is about to throw Abraham into the fire!"

We saw the Devil leading Nimrod, and a crowd piling wood onto a pyre. The Devil saw us and commanded Nimrod, "Throw those two in, too!" Nimrod ordered us to be taken, and they brought us with the Prophet Abraham next to the catapult, to cast us into the fire.

Then the Devil came to Abraham. "You claim that there is a god other than Nimrod," he observed. "Deny your claim, and I will have you saved."

I came forward. "O evil one," I exclaimed, "It is not a claim; it is the truth. And you can save no one; you can only lead people astray!"

Satan called to Nimrod, "Destroy them all!"

I threw my cloak on the ground, lifted my staff, and attacked the Devil.

The Devil saw he would have the worst of it. Screaming "Save yourself!" to Nimrod, he turned tail and ran.

I reached out with my two hands and seized the Devil in one and Nimrod in the other. Seeing that I had captured their leaders, all the soldiers fled. I took the two of them and hung them up by their feet from a tree. Adam and the hundred and twenty-four thousand prophets within him cried, "Praise be!"

Now Nimrod, his head hanging down, begged Adam to save him from me. Adam, and all those within him who are close to Allah, told me that Nimrod was not to be blamed. So I took my staff and went to Satan.

"Promise that you will never be the evil-commanding self to me!" I demanded.

"All things existing be my witness: I will never be your evil-commanding self!"

Nimrod assured me that he was ready to be my slave and to do whatever I said.

Then I felt at peace. . . .

And I saw that there was no one but I, no other guest in this temporal inn, and I said, "I am who I know I am."

And I said:

> O Lord, is the beloved within the lover?
> And the lover in the beloved?
> I find not the question why and wherefore.
> Am I one within the many?
> No, I am the one with the many in me.
> I am the owner and the owned,
> And the doer and the done.

Now I felt satisfied, for I had all I wished and I knew I could not wish for any more.

Moses appeared to me.

I said, "Oh, what a beautiful being!" and gave him salutations. He offered the same to me.

"Who are you; where do you come from?" he inquired.

"I come from Adam, and I am he."

"But where is that Adam from whom you say you come?"

"Very far away. For many thousands of years I came from Adam to Adam, but I forgot the first time I came."

"How old are you?"

"Thirteen."

"How can you be thirteen when you are that old?"

"That day when I left Eden with Adam, I lost my heart. I looked within a thousand forms and shapes to find it. I changed a thousand names, visited a thousand places for a thousand years. I became the wind with the wind and blew over land and sea. I became the waters of the rivers and poured into the sea. I became birds and beasts. I suffered thousands of pains and laughed for many a false joy. But it is only thirteen years since I found my soul within me with everything else, and it is only thirteen years since I came to know it."

"What might your name be?"

"Which of the many? For my father called me Adam, but my mother called me by many names. I lost my identity when I left my heart in Adam. When I came to Adam in this place—in each form, in each shape, in each time and each place—I was given so many names. It can neither fit in any register nor in any language."

"And what is your name?" I asked him.

"Moses, Allah's prophet, to whom He spoke."

"Then you should know my name, for Allah taught His names to His prophets."

Moses said, "So which of the names that I was taught is yours?"

"Mine is not among them," I said, "but they all come from my name."

Then Moses knew that I knew the language of the birds.

I asked Moses, "What place is this, where we were destined to meet?"

Moses said, "It is an inn where millions of heedless stay."

I saw the Pharoah arriving in great pomp and luxury, with a multitude of armies in his shape and of his flesh. With the Devil next to him as his vizier and advisor, he climbed the stairs of his high throne.

Satan spotted Moses and me. "Those two are my archenemies!" he told Pharoah, who sent his men to bring us to him.

"Would you let me speak to him?" I asked Moses.

Satan said to the Pharoah, "These two say that there is another god above you."

"Have you seen Him as you see me, that you compare Him to me?" Pharoah asked us.

"No one can see Him, but He sees all and everything without looking," Moses replied.

"This is the one who incites men against you in sorcery!" the Devil exclaimed. "Let him not speak! Punish him instantly!"

"A curse on you, dirtier than all dirt, in your ugly vanity!" I spat.

Then the Devil realized that it was I, the one he had promised to leave alone. As he tried to run, I caught him by the neck, threw him on his face, and grabbed his bag from his hand.

The Pharoah ordered his soldiers to attack me. I took my sling and kept his army at bay! The Pharoah himself fled, but before he escaped I captured his crown. I put his crown and the Devil's bag in front of Moses; Moses praised me.

The Pharoah re-formed his army and surrounded us. He sent an emissary to Moses, asking for his crown and the Devil's bag in return for our safe passage.

"Let us return to them what is theirs and save ourselves," Moses suggested.

"Let's be patient," I argued. "He's caused us enough misery! Recently, I hung him by his feet, and he promised to let me be. Let's ask him to repent for having broken his promise."

The Devil repented. We gave him back his bag and the Pharoah's crown.

As if waking from a dream, I saw that the Devil, the Pharoah, and Nimrod were the ego, the avarice, and the envy in me, and I saw that when I lose my soul, those are the ones who take me over.

Again I had found myself and security. . . .

I said, "I am the one who I know I am. I am the skies, the oceans, and the land. I am the mines of all gems. Open your eyes and know and see that both worlds are within me."

Who knows what I am talking about? It is the language of the birds. Only the king of this world and prophet of the Hereafter, Solomon, knows.

* * *

The Opening

Advice to the Ones Who Would Listen, the Ones Who Wish to Understand

O you who seek truth and the real reality, come, have pity on yourself. Find a cure for the sickness of ignorance by which you take your imagination to be reality and from which you suffer all your life. While you can, search for a cure day and night, until you feel secure from all that you fear.

You do see some people at peace, saved from the disease of ambition, though they have less than you do—while you are in pain and oppressed by all that you have.

A day will certainly come when you will regret all this, but it may be too late. Wise up now, start to learn, and leave this ignorance which you take for knowledge. Seek the company of those who have come to know the truth, and learn their language so that you understand what they say. Salvation is in a perfect human being.

After you find the perfect teacher for you, let your love for him be your guide. It is from him that you will learn to find yourself and find the truth in your own being.

Imam 'Ali (may Allah be pleased with him) asked the Messenger of Allah, "What action can I take that is not totally lost and worthless?"

The Messenger of Allah answered, "Seek truth. You will find it in yourself; therefore, know yourself. Seek the company of the wise, who know. Agree with what they say, for one understands only that with which one agrees. Be sincere in what you say—a single tongue should not speak two different words. No deceit or fraud should enter into your thoughts. Do not belittle anyone or anything, for everyone and everything in its being wishes for the same thing.

"Do not touch anything that is not yours. Avoid crowded places; even in such places, try to be with yourself, for that is the place where the truth is manifested. That is where the truth is.

"If you do all this, your sight will reach to the end of the worlds and to the end of the heavens, and you will be one and complete. Then your life will not be spent for naught, and you will be safe from temptation and pain."

O seeker of truth, the path to truth is very short. It is closer to you than your jugular vein; yet there are seventy thousand barriers—all created by you.

> The one who already knows, understands.
> What have I told the one who is heedless?
> He is not here.
> And what does the animal hear but noise?
> It either runs away or comes here.
> If you did not understand, you are not here.

Let me tell you so that you can judge yourself. If you knew, you would be with Man, not with animals shaped like men.

One day the inhabitants will leave this place. Your every cell will return to dust, and you will be left by yourself. Woe to the one who does not know himself! Then you will walk alone.

If you are a precious jewel, wherever you go they will come to your door. If you are made of rubbish, no one will want it.

Time as you know it will pass into timelessness. The cycles will be completed; the oceans will evaporate. The one who owns your soul will not look at your face, nor have compassion on you, if you are not a part of those who know Him.

O you who wish to understand, wake up from heedlessness; look at reality; admit that now you are drunk and that all you know is your imagination. If you truly seek truth, If you really wish to wake up, you must first attain the truth of dying before dying. You must die before dying in order to be alive. You must leave the imagination of this world so that you can arrive.

To learn constancy and love you have to suffer the beloved's hiding from you, and only if you are patient in suffering, will you find faith. But if you claim you are faithful already and exhibit yourself worshipping the one to whom you claim to be faithful, hoping to receive His reward, suddenly one day you may find yourself face to face with the truth that should have been worshipped; only it will be too late. You will be dead. You will regret it, but it will be of no use.

I have gone there and come back and am giving you the news. Only when your soul is in human shape can you gain or lose. Take lessons from all you see, but never say, "Why is it not another way?"

They are but bits and pieces, and they seem disconnected. Try to gather them together; your reason is the means. Be in the now, but contemplate your end.

Know that this realm has an owner and that the sultan lives in the palace of your being. Know yourself so that you will not be ashamed when you meet Him. Don't look down on anything; don't try to take someone else's share; know right from wrong, just from unjust—for the human being is built from the brick of lawful sustenance and the mortar of the advice of the wise. The human being is destroyed by that which is unlawful, by the chatter of the ignorant.

Be conscious; take advice from what you see. Listen to your conscience and talk with reason. Behave correctly even when you are by yourself. Know your place, and be humble. Kneel and sit low in the presence of the wise. Do not speak before being asked. If asked, be brief and say only that which you know. Do not be selfish. Know that the truth is with you always and everywhere. Be loyal to your friends and trustworthy to all.

Speak gently to ignorance. Be polite and quiet in the presence of wisdom. If you ask of a teacher, ask with respect. Never ask a question with an intent to test, and accept the answer and agree with it, even if it is not what you expected. If you reject, you will be rejecting yourself.

In this palace of your being there are many chambers with His secret treasures, but the palace is His. There is none other than

He. If you accept yourself as His servant, behave as a servant, but if you have become the perfect man, then you are the sultan; all is yours—and you have to keep it safe and secure.

If you do not know yourself, you are neither sultan or slave. Be prepared, then, to be put to shame and never to see the sultan of the domain. Then, you are only the dust thrown hither and thither with each breath. Hold on to the one who knows so that you know also. Otherwise, you will be disconcerted and confused.

The purpose of your coming to this world is to know yourself and to know the truth. At this stage of your eternal life you must learn to differentiate truth from falsehood. Do not spend your one and only lifetime in vain.

If you call yourself a human being, then climb to the summit of your being, where you will find reason, and begin seeking. Look at the flat lands, the steep ascents, and the pitfalls—for there are many fearful chasms—so that you will be secure from fear.

Those who are unable to discern truth from falsehood walk through this life blindly. They still run in circles today.

Each man is responsible for his own soul. For many, what they think they know is a veil preventing them from finding the secret. They ask each other, "What is this place? Who built it?" Bewildered, the blind lead the blind.

The one who feels he is high peers down and looks for it below. The one who is low looks up and seeks it above.

From the time He gathered the souls and asked them, "Am I not your Lord?" until the coming of the perfect human being, one hundred and twenty-four thousand blessed messengers came and went.

Each said one thing, and not many took heed.

Then the last blessed one came and saw the Builder within what He built, showed Him to us manifest in what He created. The one who sees, sees. What is it to the blind? If you are blind, find a guide who sees. How do the blind know if someone else sees?

The truth you seek has neither before nor after, is not in the past nor in the future. It is in the now. It has no above nor below. It is where you stand; it has neither right nor left. It is the center. It is an ocean that fits into every existence, for everything that exists is from one existence.

The ones who see anything ugly in it are rejected, because the light comes from the flame, as in a crystal chandelier where each crystal reflects the light of the same candle. All creation is but one being. Alas, they speak different tongues.

It was not my intention to give you any advice, for often the truth is told, and all who hear depart. Only the ones who are destined to hear, hear.

I do not speak of myself. It is the truth that speaks, out of compassion. The truth wills none to burn. Someone destitute with pockets full of gems, someone who refuses to put his hands in his pockets, cannot call tyrant the one who gave him the treasures, and the hands to hold them, and the mind to use them. He is the most just of the just who said:

The one who does an atom's worth of good, will see it.
The one who does an atom's worth of harm, will see it.

(Qur'an: Zilzal, 99:7)

Introduction

Shaikh Badruddin ibn Qadi Simawna, the author of *Inspirations*, is famous not only as a medieval scholar and a mystic saint but also as a revolutionary. He is held to be responsible for what was, in the fifteenth century, one of the first rebellions of the masses in history.

His father Isra'il had come from Samarkand among the many warriors and scholars of Turkistan who had entered the service of the new Ottoman state. Isra'il, a commander in the Turkish army when it crossed into Europe, was the hero who captured the fortified city of Simawna, near Edirne in what is now European Turkey. As a reward he was given the governorship of the city, and because of his great knowledge of jurisprudence, he became the *qadi*, the judge of the region.

It was in Simawna that Badruddin was born in 1358. At that time the Ottoman state was only sixty years old.

Badruddin's early education was in the hands of local scholars, Mawlana Shahidi and Yusuf, who were his father's friends. After a brief schooling in Konya, the old capital of the Seljuk Empire that had preceded the Ottomans, he was sent to Cairo.

Cairo at this time was peaceful, although wars were being mounted almost everywhere else—most notably those of the famous conqueror Timurlane and those of Yildirim Bayazid, the brash Ottoman sultan who had so rapidly expanded the frontiers of his empire.

Introduction

In Cairo young Badruddin studied philosophy, logic, law, and theology, taught by the most famous scholars of the time—Sayyid Sharif Jurjani and Mubarak Shah-i Mantiqi. And there he met a Turkish Sufi master of the Uwaysiyyah order, Shaikh Husayn Ahlati. Badruddin became Shaikh Husayn's dervish and, because of an innate talent for mysticism and high intelligence, was advanced quickly to the level of a teacher.

While Badruddin was in Egypt, Timurlane conquered Syria and arrived in Erzinjan in eastern Anatolia. From there he sent a letter to Yildirim Bayazid, asking him to pursue and arrest a large band of highwaymen who were terrorizing the people of the eastern regions. Timurlane had a weak leg, and Yildirim Bayazid was missing an eye. Timurlane wrote:

> You and I are of the same nation. I am lame and you are blind, but in spite of this, look what Allah has bestowed as His grace upon us!
>
> Let us not fight each other. Let us stay within our frontiers as kings, as friends and brothers, coexisting in peace....

Bayazid was unsympathetic and, in his answer, addressed Timurlane as *kalb akur* (mad dog).

A battle royal followed on the plain of Chubuk near Ankara. Unfortunately for Bayazid, Timurlane's forces outnumbered his by four or five to one. The Ottoman army, further hampered by the defection of its Tartar regiments, was vanquished. Yildirim Bayazid was taken prisoner, and in 1402, he died in the dungeons of the fortress in Ankara.

One of Bayazid's six sons, Musa Chelebi, stayed with his father until he died and later carried the sultan's body back to the first Ottoman capital of Bursa.

The other five sons escaped, returning to a greatly diminished Ottoman Empire, while in 1403, Timurlane returned to his capital of Tabriz and set up a glittering court, surrounding himself with scholars and artists.

To this world-famous court, Shaikh Husayn sent his dervish Badruddin.

The men of knowledge of the court of Tabriz engaged in many learned disputations, and Badruddin soon became a participant. In one scholarly debate he was made arbitrator, and it so happened that Timurlane was present. Badruddin showed such wisdom, insight, and tact that the king was very impressed. Timurlane offered him the governorship of one of his conquered provinces, the position of religious head of the empire, and his daughter's hand in marriage.

The next morning Badruddin left Tabriz in secret and went back to Cairo. He preferred being a dervish of Shaikh Husayn to being a son-in-law of the most powerful ruler of the time.

Though humbly continuing his studies in mysticism at the feet of his shaikh, Badruddin soon became well-known. Before long he was tutoring the Crown Prince Farah, son of the Egyptian king, al-Malik al-Zahir Sayfuddin Barquq.

Not long after, Shaikh Husayn died, and Badruddin was chosen to take his place. News of him spread everywhere, but he endured in Egypt as the new shaikh for only six months. At the end of half a year, escaping power and fame, he left with his wife and son to go home to Edirne.

His escape was not successful, for his reputation preceded him wherever he went, and people sought him by the thousands. On the road to Edirne he stopped in Jerusalem, Aleppo, Konya, and Tire, where he spread wisdom. Many people became his followers.

In Tire a man named Borklija Mustafa became his dervish and entered his service, never to leave him. Mustafa was a man of great worldly knowledge, extremely capable, and devoted to the shaikh. However, he was eventually to become the cause of Shaikh Badruddin's downfall.

Also while in Tire, Shaikh Badruddin received an invitation from the bishop of Chios. Chios, an island in the Aegean Sea, was then a colony of the Genoese. Shaikh Badruddin stayed ten days there as the guest of the bishop. His discourses to the Christians were translated into Greek by his steward Borklija. At the end of the visit, hundreds of Christians—including the bishop—converted to Islam and became his dervishes.

On his way home to Edirne his last stop was Kutahya in western Anatolia. One of those who entered his service there was a man called Torlak Kamal. He was destined to be another leader of the revolution attributed to Shaikh Badruddin.

When the shaikh rejoined his family in Edirne, he spent three peaceful years for himself, writing books and teaching mysticism to a relatively small group of his immediate entourage. However, these years were perhaps the most turbulent years in Ottoman history.

After the death of Yildirim Bayazid and the evacuation of Timurlane's armies from the Ottoman provinces, the empire was split into small kingdoms. From five separate capitals, the five escaped sons of the sultan fought each other for power. The contest took twelve bitter years.

Two of the most powerful sons, Mehmet Chelebi (king at Amasya) and Isa Chelebi (king at Bursa), fought each other for the regions of Anatolia. Isa Chelebi was beaten and took refuge with his oldest brother Suleyman (king at Edirne). With Suleyman's help, Isa returned to Anatolia with a strong army. Again defeated, Isa was killed at Eskishehir. In revenge Suleyman Chelebi crossed into Anatolia to fight his brother Mehmet. Caught—while drunk—in a surprise attack, he too was killed.

Musa Chelebi—the brother who had accompanied his father into prison, the brother who had actually been appointed king by Timurlane, and the only brother who had not mixed himself into these intrigues—was declared sultan in the place of Suleyman in Edirne.

During this time of vicious war and strife the people suffered, and they themselves were divided against each other. Lawlessness and disorder were widespread.

While Suleyman Chelebi reigned in Edirne, Shaikh Badruddin held no one's side and stayed out of politics. But Musa Chelebi, on becoming king, felt that the divided empire could only be reunited by re-establishing the rule of law. Knowing the reputation of Shaikh Badruddin, he insisted that he take the position of chief justice.

Along with this office, Shaikh Badruddin was given the title of Minister of Religious Affairs. Both positions were nonpolitical, but according to the Ottoman administration, came immediately after the prime minister in precedence.

For the two-and-a-half years that Shaikh Badruddin held this position, he saw to it that religious principles and religious law were supreme in every affair, applicable to the highest and lowest citizen alike. During this period he wrote his famous book on law, *Jami' al-faslayn* (Uniter of the Two Divisions).

However, in spite of his great wisdom and great religious convictions, the shaikh was unsuccessful in his attempts to correct certain of the king's actions, because Musa Chelebi was an extremely stubborn man. Finally Musa Chelebi and Mehmet Chelebi went to war. At Sofia (now in Bulgaria) Mehmet took his brother Musa prisoner and had him killed. It was the final contest. After twelve years of civil wars, the Ottoman Empire was reunited under a ruthless king.

One of the first actions of Sultan Mehmet was to replace his predecessors' administration. The usual procedure at the time was the execution, imprisonment, or exile of the previous administration's high officials, along with the confiscation of their property.

Due to the wide influence of Shaikh Badruddin, the sultan hesitated to execute him. Instead, he gave the shaikh a pension of a thousand pieces of gold per year and exiled him to Iznik.

The shaikh's two deputies, Borklija Mustafa and Torlak Kamal, accompanied him there.

This exile was very painful to Shaikh Badruddin. His conscience was clear, since he had done no wrong to anyone or to any

Introduction

principle, but his sense of justice was offended. The high position he had held had been forced upon him, and the result of his work had been exile from everything dear to him. He felt entrapped and oppressed.

While in Iznik he had a son, and he continued to write.

In the foreword of *al-Tahsil* (A Satire), a book he wrote in Iznik, he said:

> O Lord, save me from the hands of tyrants and their henchmen. Take away my pain, and, if I have erred, accord me your pardon. I am a prisoner in exile, pained, constricted, sad, enveloped in trouble. My whole being is on fire. O Lord, who brings His blessings from unexpected places, save us from all that we fear.

In exile the shaikh was visited by the deputies he had left in Egypt to represent him. They begged him to go on the Pilgrimage to Mecca and implored the local authorities to permit it. But the permission had to be obtained from the sultan himself, and Sultan Mehmet refused to grant it.

Meanwhile, Borklija Mustafa and Torlak Kamal were scheming on their own to free the shaikh from detention and to revenge the injustice done to him. They began to appeal to the populace to support him. Mustafa went to Aydin and the regions of western Anatolia. Kamal went to Kutahya. They preached the shaikh's social philosophy—the equality of all people and the right of each to a decent life corresponding to his work and productivity. However, they exaggerated Shaikh Badruddin's ideas, for they felt that any means were justified to help the shaikh. And they used the precepts of the Islamic law to defend their actions.

Thousands of supporters from among the common people gathered around them, and soon their activities became a serious challenge to the state. This news came to Shaikh Badruddin's attention. He felt further endangered, knowing that he might be held responsible for the revolt. In 1419 he managed to escape from exile. He traveled east and sought the protection of Isfandiyar Bey, ruler of a fiefdom in Kastamonu in central Anatolia. His intention was to escape to Samarkand, to the land of his ancestors.

Isfandiyar Bey, fearing the reprimand of the sultan, did not permit him to go to Central Asia. He let him depart on a boat from Sinop, apparently bound for Crimea. The captain had orders to bring Shaikh Badruddin to the Ottoman provinces of Europe, where he was forced ashore.

Trying to hide, Shaikh Badruddin passed from city to city, but his name, as always, managed to precede him. Wherever he went, thousands of people met and followed him. Rather than achieving obscurity, he appeared to be gathering followers.

At that time the Ottoman armies, under the sultan's son Murat Bey, were fighting in the west to capture Salonika from the Greeks. Nevertheless, because of the danger of a popular revolt and civil war, the sultan ordered Murat Bey to lead his forces away from the battlefield and against Borklija Mustafa and Torlak Kamal. As a result, both men were caught and executed.

In the aftermath, Shaikh Badruddin was arrested in Serez (Serrai, near Salonika). He was brought to the sultan to be judged. In a chronicle, called *Menakip-name*, this encounter is recorded:

> The sultan: "You look pale, your skin has grown yellow. Why couldn't you have settled somewhere and minded your own business?"
>
> Badruddin: "The sun appears yellow near the time of its setting."
>
> The sultan: "Why have you opposed your masters?"
>
> Badruddin: "Why have you opposed truth and justice?"
>
> The sultan: "What injustice have I done to you?"

Introduction

Badruddin: "I asked your permission to go to the Holy Pilgrimage, which Allah requires of me. So you opposed Him and His prescriptions, while I had to obey Him. I left you and went to Isfandiyar Bey for protection and freedom."

The sultan had gathered judges and scholars as a jury to decide on the fate of the shaikh. Most of the discussion among the jurors was about the ideas the shaikh expressed in this present work, *Inspirations*. They claimed that some of these ideas were blasphemous.

Finally, one of the scholars, a Persian called Fakhruddin Ajami, proposed the execution of the shaikh, based on the following rationale: "When your affairs are centered around one man and someone comes to divide the unity, kill him."

Shaikh Badruddin responded to his condemnation thusly:

If you claim that, because I have left my obedience to the rules of the sultan, I have left my attachment to Islam by my own intent and actions—I accept your religious politics!

In Serez, in the year 1420, on the twenty-seventh of the Islamic month of Shawwal, Shaikh Badruddin was executed by hanging at the age of sixty-two.

Later, a large tomb was erected for him. It became a shrine visited by many Sufis. In recent times, after the independence of Greece, this tomb was destroyed. In 1924 Shaikh Badruddin's remains were brought to Istanbul, and they are now buried near the tomb of Sultan Mahmud the Just.

To succeeding generations, *Inspirations*, Shaikh Badruddin's most important work on mysticism, has been as controversial as the political incidents that affected his life.

His position as a jurist, philosopher, and grammarian is

universally accepted and praised. His contemporaries, themselves famous scholars—Ibn Arab-shah and his teacher Sayyid Sharif Jurjani—claimed him to be "the ocean of knowledge in jurisprudence" and "perfection in logic and wisdom." But his ideas on theology and mysticism, as expressed in *Inspirations*, were not only used against him during his trial but were also condemned for hundred of years after his death.

Many venerable shaikhs have spoken against him. Shaikh Bali of Sofia (d. 1553) gave this posthumous judgment on him to Sultan Suleyman the Magnificent: "Shaikh Badruddin, cursed by Allah, received His Wrath by being hanged." The famous saint Shaikh Aziz Mahmud Huda'i (d. 1628) presented his judgment to Sultan Ahmed I, calling him "a heretic and a libertine who tried to make unlawful into lawful, and in his book *Inspirations*, denied the signs of the Day of Judgment and the Resurrection." Shaikh Nuruddin Zadi (d. 1573) also attacked Badruddin for the unconventional ideas about the Resurrection which he expressed in *Inspirations*.

On the other hand, Shaikh Muslahuddin Yavusi, the father of the famous jurist Abus-Su'ud, defended Shaikh Badruddin. He explained and justified Badruddin's concept of the Resurrection—which denies the material reappearance of mankind on the Day of Judgment—saying: "When no man will be left alive there will be a renewed creation of Adam from earth and water, and from him mankind will be reproduced again, to be present on the Day of Judgment."

In *Inspirations*, Shaikh Badruddin interprets many essential concepts of Islamic theology in a very original and personal way. For instance, he does not admit the Divine essence of the Creator to be separate from the creation. He considers eternity to be connected to the existence of the universe, as the soul, Paradise, Hell, and the angels are all created and a part of the universe. Hell is nothing other than the effect of spiritual pain produced by wrong-doings, and Paradise nothing but the peace and joy that are the effect of right actions. Following Ptolemy's astronomy, he seeks the eight

Introduction

gates of Paradise and the seven gates of Hell in heavenly bodies. According to him, angels and devils are only the influences which lead man to truth on one hand, or to temptations and deceptions, on the other.

The question of destiny, which is so important in Islam—and which is one of the concepts the discussion of which is discouraged by the Qur'an—becomes a central theme in the shaikh's philosophy. He says that the will of Allah is the actualization of the predisposition of things and that Allah will not change this predisposition.

He refutes the conventional signs of the coming of the end of the world. In fact he does not separate this world and the Hereafter. He considers the differences between life and afterlife to be theoretical, nominal, and relative, and he admits no separation of the physical being from the spiritual being, which he considers parallel and coincident. For him, temporal and eternal are the same. The signs of the imminent end of the world both did not and will not happen, and/or are always happening.

In his last chapter, which concerns the prophet Jesus (upon him be peace), he argues that Jesus (upon him be peace) is dead, but has always existed and will always exist in spirit. This also is the case of the perfect man.

Man in the beginning—in a time which Shaikh Badruddin calls the period of ignorance—was a pagan and worshipped concrete idols. When he is introduced to religion he is no different, except that he worships idols of the imagination. Hope reposes in Allah's manifestation of truth to him and in him; then man becomes a servant and serves as he was meant to, and as a good servant, he acts upon the orders he receives from his Lord.

The perfect man, given the ears to hear truth, will receive inspirations, *waridat*, which he cannot help but obey and carry out. The salvation of the unperfected is in following such men. They will then profit from the services and the actions of the perfect man.

The many people who believed in Shaikh Badruddin's point of

view hoped to reap the social benefits the Shaikh had promised. His liberal thought and attitudes indeed softened prevailing prejudices—the hard-line distinction between lawful and unlawful, the harsh treatment of the sinful, the supposed inferiority of the Christian and Jewish minorities. He considered that all men were equal and that the whole creation was for their benefit, to be enjoyed by them in common. These ideas attracted many Christians and Jews as well as Turks. Thousands of poor people, as well as discontented former officials who had lost their high offices, gathered around him.

It was not Shaikh Badruddin who was responsible for the revolution forever attached to his name. His reputation was due to the short-sighted worldly application of his ideas, as propagated by the ambitious among his followers, and the chaotic times in which he lived.

His desire to live a quiet, secluded life was proven by his flights from power—from worldly power at the court of Timurlane and from religious power in Egypt as the heir of his shaikh. Finally, in Edirne, he was cornered; there was no place else to run, and his public destiny could no longer be avoided. Shaikh Badruddin's acceptance of martyrdom is a confirmation of the Prophetic precept:

> The faithful one is he who, when he encounters a wrong, tries to set it right by his hand. If he cannot, he tries to set it right by his words. If he cannot, he wishes for it to be changed. The one who does not care and does not even wish for the wrong to be remedied, lacks faith even as much as a grain of mustard seed.

On Sufism

The basis of all the mystical paths of Islam is the idea of unity—the concept of the oneness of being, of all existence.

This belief in the oneness of all existence originated in ancient oriental philosophy. It existed not only in India and China but among the ancient Akkadians, Sumerians, Assyrians, Chaldeans, Persians, and Egyptians. From these peoples it passed to the Phoenicians and to classical Greece. It found its ultimate deployment in Islam during the 'Abbasid period, when the mystical paths called *tariqahs* in Arabic and known as Sufi sects in the West, first appeared in an organized fashion.

But mysticism and the sense of oneness of being was not suddenly infused into Islam with the classical heritage, as has sometimes been proposed. It was always there. It is nothing more, or other than, the practice of the truth of Islam. The intuition of truth present in so many traditions was distilled to its essence by Islam, then embodied in a vehicle perfectly suited to it. The Sufi sects arose to ensure that this union of soul and body would never be sundered.

The final goal of Sufism is the unification of apparent multiplicity with the Essential Oneness. According to Sufi teaching, this is only possible through the annihilation of all appearances— and, above all, of the appearance of one's self—in Allah.

There are three steps in this process.

The first is *la ma'buda illa Llah*—"there is none worthy of worship other than Allah."

The second is *la maqsuda illa Llah*—"there is no purpose or goal but Allah."

The third is *la mawjuda illa Llah*—"nothing exists but Allah."

At the first level of "there is none worthy of worship other than Allah," though multiplicity is reduced to the worshipped and the worshipper, one is still guilty of the sin of duality, of attributing partners to Allah—for the whole world still appears to exist, as does the worshipper.

At the second level of "there is no purpose or goal but Allah," the problem still remains. Though Allah becomes the only object of one's wish, in the denial of other objects their existence is still implied—and one's self is still there.

True unity is only attained at the third level of "nothing exists but Allah." Thus the goal must be not merely the rejection of multiplicity from desire and perception but also finding one's being solely within the only Everlasting One.

The origin and the cause of perfection is Allah, the only existence. The cause of all deficiency and evil is man, who does not exist. All good and perfection belong to Allah, who is permanent. Evil and deficiency are fleeting in experience and nonexistent in reality. The temporal is like a current of air. True being can only be eternal. The unity of being is the disappearance of the temporal in the eternal.

In Islamic mysticism the seeker attempts to reach this goal of unity in a system of education consisting of four steps.

The first period of education is called the teaching of negation and affirmation. During this time the novice recites and concentrates on the Divine declaration *la ilaha illa Llah* (There is no god but Allah).

The second period of education is called purity and consolidation. Now the student recites and concentrates on the phrase *illa Hu*, "none other than He"—*Hu* (He) being the perfect name of Allah.

The third phase is called *fana' fi-Llah*, "losing oneself in Allah," an advanced state during which the practiced student invokes and seeks *al-Haqq* (the Absolute Truth).

The final state is the level of *baqa' bi-Llah*, "existing in Allah." To exist in Allah is the state of the perfect man, where there is no longer a seeker of truth, for the seeker has become the Truth.

This system is parallel to the three degrees of knowledge. The first is *'ilm al-yaqin*, knowledge obtained indirectly through information supported by rational proof. The second is *'ayn al-yaqin*, knowledge acquired through direct experience. The third is *haqq al-yaqin*—annihilation of all knowledge, including the sense of one's existence, in Allah, and existing in Truth, becoming the Truth.

According to Malamiyyah all attributes, all actions, relate and belong solely to Allah. There is no existence other than He. All and everything is included by and disappears within this single Being. The final goal is to realize the disappearance in Him and to be one with Him.

On Malamiyyah

The word *Malamiyyah* comes from the Arabic root *malama*, meaning to reproach, to blame, to punish. Malamiyyah is a Sunni sect of dervishes who subject themselves to public reproach by appearing to disregard the rules of proper behavior, even the outward rites of religion.

In reality a Malami's goal is to lead a moral and devout life serving Allah's creation for His sake alone. Privately he discounts all his good deeds and counts only his failings and errors as his own actions. He believes that since all good coming from him is not his but belongs to Allah alone, it should be kept a secret, while he publicizes his wrongdoings in an exaggerated way as terrible sins. He is willing to receive the reproach, the blame, and even the harshest punishment for them.

This behavior is the principle, the discipline of Malamiyyah. To attract the disapproval and anger of the world against himself is an attempt to enlist the public as his ally in his battle against his ego. His aim is to crush his arrogance and to expose his hypocrisy.

According to Islam the purpose of the creation of the human being is to serve Allah. Human beings can only serve Him if they know Him and are together with Him. The meaning of true obedience is to be in harmony with the one whom one serves. Humanity has all that it needs for this purpose, for Allah has taught

On Malamiyyah

Adam (upon him be peace) all His Names and bestowed upon humankind His Divine Attributes.

Man is designed to be the extension of Allah's beneficence upon the universe: thus all good coming from man belongs to Allah. To assume credit for good actions is hypocrisy, for it is to claim something as one's own that one does not possess. And to attribute to oneself that which belongs to Allah amounts to the only sin considered unforgivable in Islam—*shirk*, the assigning of partners to Allah.

Man is also given another quality which exists in none other in the creation. It is will, the ability to choose. He can either choose to be in harmony with Divine harmony and live in accordance with truth (thus reaching the highest level possible, that of servanthood to Allah), or he may in arrogance, in the revolt against the truth, opt for the lie of his own fantasies of himself as reality.

It is only man who can try to claim to be lord and owner of himself and the world, who can try to claim that other men are his servants. But arrogance, lying and revolt are the characteristics of the devil, whose role is to draw us away from our own nature. Truth is natural; it is reality. Lying is unnatural; it is imagination.

The devil's partner in each of us is the ego. Thus the Malami fights by every means against the tempting imaginings of the evil-commanding ego—the ego that hides the lie under the guise of the truth, the ugly under the cosmetics of beauty. When the Malami excludes all his good deeds from recognition, he exposes the inner evil in all its ugly nudity. The angry reactions of the public strengthen him, for he feels that he has succeeded in recruiting the help of his environment in the battle against his domineering ego. Furthermore, he also believes that he is helping his own accusers, perhaps to see in themselves the same faults which they criticize in him. Yet he is very careful not to be critical of his accusers.

The Malami holds that whoever praises him is his enemy, for he acts as the friend of his archenemy, while whoever chastises him is his friend, for he is the enemy of his archenemy.

Malamiyyah is a form of asceticism which is practiced in public rather than in seclusion. It is an outward, active form of asceticism—an attempt at total heedfulness of oneself and one's actions, a full acceptance of accountability for one's wrongdoings. The actions of the Malamiyyah are reasoned and responsible. They know that they are sacrificing their respectability, their acceptability by the public, when they erase from their behavior all insincerity, and all signs of piety, which they consider to be hypocrisy and arrogance.

Theirs is a pessimistic outlook on their worldly existence, which they see as tainted by the temptations of the ego. Their response is to deprive that ego of all that feeds it—not only from worldly desires of the flesh but even from acquiring knowledge and from public manifestation of their worship and devotion, all of which may be the ego's desire to be rewarded.

In doing this they sacrifice all ordinary pleasure, joy, and satisfaction—for Allah's sake. However, for the sake of other people they would give up their property, their comfort, even their lives. This principle of self-sacrifice is one of the dominant characteristics of Malamiyyah. It came to be known as *futuwwah*, which, as either a system or a principle of mystical knighthood, involved helping and serving others to the detriment of one's own material existence.

The Malami, who wishes to weaken his ego, denies it anything which feeds it. Abandoning the objects of material desire, he relinquishes them to the ones who are in need, giving up his property, his sustenance, his knowledge, his physical abilities, his strength—even his life.

Hadrat Muhyiddin Ibn 'Arabi (may his secret be sanctified) praises Malamiyyah in his *Futuhat al-Makiyyah*:

> The Malamis, who are also called the ones who expose their blameworthiness, make the literal meaning of "blame" appear weak in comparison to their actions.

They are the guides of the path leading to Allah. The Master of the Universe is among them, none other than the Messenger of Allah, the Prophet Muhammad, peace and blessings upon him.

These are the ones who have established upon the face of this world Allah's injunctions of what is right and what is wrong. They have shown them in actions. They have explained the reasons they have left what belongs to the world to the world and what belongs to the hereafter to the hereafter. They look upon the material world as if they are outside of it, as the Lord looks upon His creation. They have not confused the Truth with the imagination of the Truth.

Malamiyyah as such is not an organized mystical sect, with congregations, centers, particular rites, costumes, etc. It is a way of life; it is a basic faith, a heroic attitude. It is a faith for leading a healthy, peaceful, successful life: perfect health is secured by interior purity; peace is obtained through a clear conscience; and the greatest of all success is victory over the tyranny of the evil-commanding ego.

The Malami's Attitude Toward Evil and Hypocrisy

Ego and hypocrisy are the two enemies of all Sufis and, most actively, of the Malamis. They believe ego to be a material entity that places itself in the center of man. Ego is the cause of all evil, while the center of man is the rightful house of the soul, which is usurped by the ego.

The soul, the direct opposite of the ego, is the source of beauty and good. There are also two other forces within man: the heart and the Sacred Secret.

The four active ingredients—the soul, the ego, the heart, and the Secret (sometimes called Reason)—compete with and complement each other during each person's lifetime.

Each of them has a different function. The soul is the source of life; the ego, the source of desires; the heart, the source of Divine knowledge; the Secret (or the mind), the source of perception and conception. The soul generates the energy for life and good actions. The ego creates the fire for ambition and wrongdoings. The heart is the center of love and the yearning for God. The mind seeks and retains knowledge. If the heart leans towards the ego, it assumes its characteristics of ambition, pleasure, and immorality. If it leans towards the soul, it assumes its attributes of decency, purity, and love of good. The Secret, the mind, watches and records. The soul, the ego, and the heart do not see the Secret, but it sees them—yet it has no power to judge or to influence.

(The Sufis also believe in the Secret of the Secret, which only Allah knows. They consider it to be His eye within every human being.)

According to the Malamis, there are four forms of worship, corresponding to the four centers.

They view the outward rites of religion as the worship of the ego, performed by the body and the tongue (reciting prayers, prostrating, and so forth). Its purpose is to seek the approval of God and man, in the hope of receiving the benefits of this world and the hereafter.

The prayer of the heart is in the remembrance of and thankfulness for the Divine blessings, in being aware of Allah's attributes in His creation.

The devotion of the soul is the realization of the oneness of all and everything—which is in Allah—and the acceptance of one's nothingness. That is the level which the Sufis call losing oneself in Allah.

It is at this point that the worship of the Sacred Secret begins. In awe—without words, actions, or feelings—it reflects like a mirror the real reality, the Truth.

These different levels of worship follow in sequence. One leads to the other. The person at a lower level should aspire to the next higher level. However, the later level does not remove the necessity of observing and practicing the earlier one. To worship with an inner devotion of the heart, feeling Allah's blessings and attributes, does not negate doing one's ritual prayers. In fact, if the devotion of the heart appears, it appears within the ritual prayer when one is able to exclude the ego. And if the ego slips back, rather than be ruined entirely, devotion will then merely revert to the outward prayer of ego, which is the lowest form of worship. Still, if this happens, it is a deplorable decrease of state.

One must be extremely cautious of two things. One is that the aspiration for a higher level not lead to the false imagination of being at a higher level. The other is that the memory of a former level not pull one down from a genuinely higher level.

For instance, someone who has reached the level of the Sacred Secret will lose his cognizance of the truth if he remembers his state at the level of the soul, where he had lost himself in Allah. On the other hand, if someone who is worshipping in the state of the heart imagines himself in the state of the Sacred Secret, the imagination of awe will prevent him from truly seeing Allah's attributes in His creation and His blessings upon him. These confusions are considered by the Malamis as the most dangerous kind of hypocrisy.

The Malami way of life is a realistic one, relating every happening to the different centers and dealing with every situation with the appropriate center. To let the heart deal with the affairs of the ego, or the ego with the affairs of the soul, is what they call hypocrisy.

Sincerity is the means of combating hypocrisy. Yet seldom is it mentioned in the vocabulary of the Malami, for sincerity is the path which leads to the union with God through total obedience, and the Malami feels unworthy. The Melami way is the path leading to the path of sincerity. By correcting their actions and appearance with total disregard for public acceptance—even to the extent of making their acceptable behavior appear obnoxious to the public—the Malamis eliminate all possibility of self-satisfaction or vainglory.

It may be said that all the principles of Malamiyyah are based on the accusation of one's self. In fact the words *ithm* (accusation) and *malam* (blame) are the same in their view. If they feel love towards someone, they do their best to make the loved one hate them. Yet, if they see the traces of the same faults in others for which they blame themselves, they praise those people. For all qualities and faults are to be discounted, since they are the dictates of the all-commanding ego. The truth is only with Allah and from Allah. All creation is under His will. All that happens is one's destiny. Therefore, all that one does has no personal value.

They say that to attribute value to one's actions and claim them as one's own is pride. To eliminate pride, it suffices to realize that one is created from a blood clot, that one's life is nothing more than what happens to a piece of straw, moving hither and thither in the violent sea of this world, and that one ends as a stinking corpse, disgusting even to one's friends.

They go as far as proposing that even the worship of the Lord has nothing to do with the worshipper, for if one considers even one's faith in Allah as one's own, one is trying to match wills with the Lord.

They quote the saint Bayazid Bistami: "The thickest veils between man and Allah are the wise man's wisdom, the worshipper's worship, and the devotion of the devout." He also said: "If I only knew that I had taken one single step in sincerity, I would give no value to anything else."

In all their heroic actions of self-reproach, sacrifice, and public punishment, their strategy is one of pessimism and pain. They have even forbidden themselves to shed tears, believing that it might ease that intentional pain.

In contrast to this self-imposed affliction, they are very indulgent toward the faults and negativity of others, especially when directed toward themselves. Why accuse anyone else? Such accusation only lets two egos clash. They try to look upon others with the eye of truth, seeing their behavior as a manifestation of their destiny and not of their own doing.

Obviously all of this hard discipline has the purpose of advancing their spiritual state; yet when a purer spiritual state was observed, it was their policy to fear and doubt it and to increase their self-condemnation, for they considered their own perception of such states to be a test. They hid their spiritual elevation, thus increasing their humbleness, their pain, their fear. Abu Amr ibn Muja'id, a Malami, said:

> If one does not consider every sign of spiritual inspiration as hypocrisy, every heightened spiritual state as claiming something which is not one's own, one will not have the slightest taste of sincerity.

They believe that the purity that sincerity brings is a secret trust and should be kept as such. Thus they quote the tradition of the Prophet Muhammad (peace and blessings be upon him), who said:

> I asked my Lord about sincerity. He said, "It is a secret that I entrust to the hearts of My beloved servants."

They consider the secret that Allah entrusts to be a hidden thing that human conscience should be jealous to show to anyone but Allah.

Abu Zakariya al-Sanji said:

> A spiritual state is a trust entrusted to its owner.
> If it is divulged, the owner is not worthy of trust.

It is the fear of divulging that Secret trust which prevents them from public rituals and public teaching. Fearing that their control might be weakened in a state of ecstasy and that they might expose their state, they prefer silence to instruction, especially with the uninitiated. Yet they do teach the basic principles of Islam, and the traditions of the Prophet Muhammad (peace and blessings be upon him) and the canonic law. In this case they feel that they are teaching that which is already known.

They also guard as their secret the inspirational knowledge

which comes by means of their Shaikh, which they consider divine and given to whomever Allah has destined. Knowledge is a part of one's destiny, just as is what happens to one and what happens through one. All of this is temporal, and none of it belongs to any individual. Abu Bakr Muhammad ibn 'Ali ibn Ja'far al-Kittani (d. 935/323 H) said:

> How can anyone think that his knowledge is his own, when neither did he make it, nor can he do anything with it, nor can he keep it!

Knowledge is also a trust from Allah. As they keep their states a secret, so do the Malamis keep secret their vast knowledge and spiritual experience. That is why what is generally known about them derives from their negative outward appearance.

The History of Malamiyyah

1. The First Phase

Although Malamiyyah—understood as the principle of asceticism within society—existed in many ancient spiritual disciplines, it took the famous early renunciate shaikh Hamdun al-Qassar of Nishapur (d. 883-4/271 H) to make it into an Islamic mystical profession.

Hamdun, celebrated for his knowledge as well as his austerity, followed the school of Imam Sufyan al-Thawri in canon law and was a disciple of Abu Turab al-Nakhshabi in Sufism. His fame spread from Nishapur (in Persia) to Baghdad, where he received high praise from some of the most lastingly influential Sufi shaikhs. The great Junayd al-Baghdadi (d. 909-910/297 H), the pivotal master through whom nearly all the *tariqahs* trace their lineage, said, "If anyone would have been worthy to be a prophet after Allah sealed prophethood with Muhammad (peace and blessings of Allah be upon him), it would have been Hamdun."

A recent Malami, Sadiq Wijdani, said:

> Hamdun reached the state of purity, the truth, and the level of oneness through his great battle with his ego, by hiding his state, although he was the

truth itself appearing as humble earth, and by running away from arrogance and hypocrisy as one runs from lions. He became an example of how men should live their lives.

We can learn about this early, illustrious Melami through his sayings and from anecdotes about him. Wijdani quotes Shaikh Hamdun:

> If one does not see his own ego as worse then the ego of the Pharaoh, he is proud indeed!

> *

> If you see a staggering drunkard on the street, imitate him, so that your arrogance will not lead you to condemn him—for easily you also could be like him.

> *

> Don't divulge to others the secrets entrusted to you.

> *

> If anyone has a sign of good in him, keep his company. Certainly you will benefit from that good.

> *

> To be satisfied with your lot is to hold onto your Lord.

> *

> The devil and his minions are delighted with three things: a believer killing a believer, a person dying without faith, and the fear of poverty in the human heart.

Inspirations

Qushayri, in his monumental *Risalah*, mentions that 'Abdullah ibn Manazil asked for advice from Hamdun al-Qassar. Hamdun said:

> If you are able, do not care about anything in this world. Above all do not get angry that something is not as it should be, and ask yourself, "Do I have the power to change it?"

Perhaps the most famous story of Shaikh Hamdun is this:

> A very close friend of Hamdun was on his deathbed. The shaikh stayed with him until his last breath. As the man died, Hamdun blew out the candle.
>
> The other people present exclaimed, "At a time like this, more light is called for!" He replied, "Before, the candle was his. Now it belongs to his heirs!"

From the example of Hamdun, Malamiyyah spread quickly—in a quarter of a century—among the Turcomans of rural Khurasan and the citizens of Nishapur in Persia, and in the cities of Herat and Kabul in what is now Afghanistan. Soon Baghdad too became a center. Great teachers such as Ahmad Khadruyah, Junayd, 'Abdullah al-Murta'ish, Ahmad ibn Yahya al-Jalla, and their numerous students made Baghdad into a spearhead of Malamiyyah. From Baghdad the teaching spread to Mosul and Aleppo in Syria, where, much later, it was still strong enough to affect the great Syrian shaikhs of the seventh Islamic century, such as Shaikh Rislani Dimashqi and Abul-Hasan 'Ali al-Hariri.

Malamiyyah was already the principal influence on the Turkic Sufi sects that were being established in the fourth, fifth, and sixth Islamic centuries. It even influenced the world-famous founder of the Mawlawiyyah *tariqah*, Mawlana Jelaluddin Rumi—partially through Baha'uddin Walad (his father and the deputy of the Persian visionary Najmuddin Kubra), but especially through his inspirer, the enigmatic Shams al-Tabrizi. The relationship of the Malami approach and the Mawlawi tariqah proved to be enduring and is visible in the works of later teachers and poets such as Neshati Ahmad Dede, Jawri, Nahifi, Fasih.

Malamiyyah's attraction for the Turkic peoples persists in our own times. Among the peasants of Anatolia and other Turkish-speaking regions, when one mentions the saints, even now it is assumed they came from Khurasan. Ordinary people have been powerfully impressed by the reputation of the early Malami saints of Nishapur—knights in the greatest battle, the war against the evil of arrogance, hypocrisy, and egotism; humble warriors without armor who sacrificed all they possessed, even their lives, for the victory of sincerity and truth.

2. The Second Phase

Malamiyyah entered its second phase in Turkey, in the eighth Islamic century, with the saint Hajji Bayram Wali and his disciple, Amir Siqqini.

Hajji Bayram Wali was one of the greatest native Turkish Sufis. Born in 1352/753 H in the village of Solfasil near Ankara, he was the son of a humble farmer, but as a young man he became the head of the Kara Medrese in Ankara. (In early Ottoman times many such universities, left by the earlier Seljuk dynasty, were to be found in the cities of Anatolia. Distinguished scholars such as Mullah Fenari, Ibn Malak, Dawud Kayseri, and Shaikh Shahabuddin Sivasi taught at these centers. So, although we do not know anything about Hajji Bayram's early education, we know he must have been just such a prominent scholar.)

Inspirations

Soon, however, he abandoned his university teaching and entered the mystic path under Shaikh Hamiduddin Aksarayi in the distant city of Bursa, first capital of the Ottoman Empire. Teacher and disciple traveled together in Syria and the Hijaz.

When Hamiduddin Aksarayi passed away in 1412-13/815 H, Hajji Bayram Wali, who was his deputy, took his place. He established a new mystic sect joining the two major *tariqahs* of the time, Khalwatiyyah and Naqshbandiyyah. The new path was called Bayramiyyah after its founder, and it proved to be wildly popular. It spread with lightning speed from the city of Ankara (where Hajji Bayram had again settled) throughout central Anatolia.

Government authorities as well as some influential leaders of orthodox Islam were worried about the size and possible social consequences of this very large movement. They suspected political motives, and informed the sultan. Consequently, in order to investigate him, Sultan Murad II invited Hajji Bayram to Edirne (which had meanwhile become the new capital of the Empire). At their first meeting, however, the sultan realized that all the allegations were false. He rewarded Hajji Bayram lavishly and sent him on his way.

Among the honors and gifts the sultan showered upon the shaikh was an edict absolving all the shaikh's dervishes from state obligations, including taxes. This advantage further increased the number of people claiming attachment to the shaikh—and a serious decrease in the treasury of the state was the result!

Responding to complaints, the sultan sent the shaikh a request: "Would the venerable saint Hajji Bayram please apprise us of the number and names of his adherents?"

(Now, the teaching of Hajji Bayram Wali was certainly opposed to taking advantage of anyone. His principle was to serve society rather than to profit from it. He assigned the greatest importance to moral action in the world. He held such action in much more esteem than thoughts, knowledge, or spiritual states.

In fact, when one of his most beloved dervishes, Mehmet Bijan, wrote a wonderful book on the Prophet Muhammad (peace and blessings be upon him) and asked his opinion, he told him, "My son, if you had fed the heart and body of someone, it would have been a better deed than the writing of this book!"

Hajji Bayram's rule was that his disciples must teach what they had learned as they had learned it, without any compensation. They were instructed to take up a trade suitable to their abilities, and if they earned more than their humble lives required, to give the rest to the needy. Hajji Bayram Wali personally farmed with his own hands, personally brought in the harvest with his students. Communally they collected the excess and distributed it to the poor. The saying, "The hand at work, the heart with Allah," is from him. The saying, "To serve the people is to serve the Lord, for the creation is the child of the Creator" is also from him. He advised statesmen to rule with justice and generosity and did not permit government officials to enter his sect, for he feared they would neglect their duties to the public.)

When Hajji Bayram received the message from the sultan asking the number and names of his followers, he asked all his dervishes to gather on a certain day in a large field in Ankara. Tens of thousands of people came together. Hajji Bayram Wali, dressed all in white, stood on a hill in front of a white tent and said, "I have received orders from my Lord to sacrifice some of my dervishes. Whoever wants to give his life, come forward!"

After a moment, one man walked up to him. The shaikh took him into the tent. Outside, the crowd saw a sudden rush of blood—for inside, unseen, the shaikh had slaughtered a ram!

Hajji Bayram left the first volunteer hidden in the tent, and with his clothes stained red, he came out and asked for the next sacrifice. Horrified, everyone remained motionless and silent.

As the shaikh repeated his request, one old woman came forward. "Let my life be your sacrifice!" she said. The shaikh led her inside, and the same scene was repeated.

When Hajji Bayram came out of the tent and asked for the next volunteer, voices cried, "Our shaikh has lost his mind! He will kill us all! Let's run away!" And the whole assembly dissolved.

Hajji Bayram then wrote the sultan, "All I have are one and a half dervishes!" With this, he declined the sultan's favors to his followers.

Later Sufis understood that the one whole dervish was the second volunteer, the old woman, who came forward despite the evidence of death—while the half dervish was the first volunteer, who had no proof of what the shaikh would do!

When Hajji Bayram Wali was on his deathbed, one of his ranking deputies, Akshamsuddin, stayed very close to him, hoping to be appointed his successor. (Akshamsuddin would later become the teacher of the young Sultan Mehmet, who conquered Constantinople in 1453/857 H.) Meanwhile a humble dervish, Amir Siqqini, who gained his sustenance through making knives, remained standing at the door of the room.

The shaikh would open his eyes and say, "I am thirsty—bring me water!" All the dervishes present would rush to bring him a glass. Each time the shaikh refused to drink and poured the water into a pot of flowers. Finally Amir Siqqini brought him a glass. Hajji Bayram Wali drank, and leaving some drops in the glass, he passed it back to the young dervish, saying, "Drink, for this is my secret trust unto you!"

Then, knowing the rivalry between his two disciples, he declared, "Nothing but fire will decide the difference between Amir Siqqini and Akshamsuddin!" And so he died in 1429-30/833 H, at the age of eighty.

The History of Malamiyyah

With the master gone, Akshamsuddin indeed succeeded as head of the Bayramiyyah, but Amir Siqqini was troubled. Those who followed Akshamsuddin established themselves in an organized fashion according to what was expected of *tariqahs* at the time: they founded formal rituals and took on specific costumes, customs, and outward manners, such as kissing the hand of the shaikh and prostrating in front of him.

At first Amir Siqqini attended these ceremonies, but he never participated in them. One day, Akshamsuddin chastised him for not taking part. He said, "If you are not with us, then I will take the turban and the garb of our sect away from you!"

Siqqini said, "Do you truly believe that you can take them from me?"

Akshamsuddin said, "Certainly I can, and I have the authority."

Siqqini said, "Then come to my house after the Friday congregation, and if Allah permits we will see if you are able to strip the signs of the dervish life from me! Bring our brothers as witnesses."

On Friday Akshamsuddin and the congregation came to Amir Siqqini's house. In front of the house they found a flaming fire! Siqqini, dressed in his dervish garb, called to the crowd.

"I dare you to enter this fire with me!" he said. "If the mark of wisdom, sincerity, and closeness to Allah is in these clothes, then they will not burn. If the purity of love and nothingness are in ourselves, then we will not be touched by the fire!" And saying, "In the name of Allah, the Beneficent, the Merciful!" he walked into the blaze.

The crowd watched in awe as Amir Siqqini whirled and smiled in the flames, while his turban, his garments, and his staff all burned to ashes—everything but a shawl that Hajji Bayram Wali had given him with his own hands. Wrapping that around himself, he came out of the fire.

Remembering what their shaikh had predicted about the

resolution of their differences, Akshamsuddin and Amir Siqqini embraced each other and were reconciled.

From that date on, however, Bayramiyyah split in two. The followers of Amir Siqqini came to be known as Malamiyyah-Siddiqiyyah. They wore no special clothes to differentiate them from other people, assumed no distinguishing signs, and established no buildings or centers of their own. Their only sign was poverty, humbleness, trustworthiness, and beneficence. In this way they became a secret society, for they could not be told apart from ordinary people by any outward mark.

3. The Present Phase

The most recent development of Malamiyyah began in the nineteenth century, with Sayyid Muhammad Nur al-'Arabi, born in Egypt in 1813/1228 H.

Nur al-'Arabi's family was originally from Jerusalem; Sufi practice was their domestic tradition. The child, orphaned at three, was adopted by his maternal uncle and at the age of seven sent to al-Azhar, the famous religious school in Cairo. Already a novice to Shaikh Hasan al-Quwayni at sixteen, at twenty-seven he traveled to Yanya, now in Bulgaria, and became a dervish in the Naqshbandi *tariqah*. Nine months later, at his shaikh's orders, he went to Mecca to perform the Pilgrimage. He stayed there a year to study, and while in Mecca, he became a member of the Khalwati-Sha'bani and Uwaysi Sufi orders as well. Then he returned to Egypt, to his first shaikh, Hasan al-Quwayni.

His shaikh gave him the right to teach and sent him to the European regions of the Ottoman Empire. Finally he settled in Skopia (now in Yugoslavia) as a theology professor at the Hifzi Pasha Medrese.

These regions at the time were centers of Malamiyyah, and it is known that the discipline that Nur al-'Arabi used in his teaching had more of the characteristics of Malamiyyah than of the strict rites of Naqshbandiyyah.

During the ten years that he lived on and off in the European parts of the Empire, he exercised great influence and gathered thousands of people around him. The proof of this is the fact that in 1843/1259 H, when he decided to go on the Pilgrimage again, 470 of his dervishes accompanied him.

His humbleness was evident when he declared, on arrival in Mecca, "The knowledge we have acquired suffices us not. Certainly in the blessed city of Mecca there is a perfect teacher, whom we must find and from whom we must learn."

And, indeed, on that trip he found a man who was known as Dervish Mehmet of Mecca, "mad with Allah." He relates:

> After circumambulating the Ka'bah I sat to meditate. A person who appeared to be a madman came and sat next to me, his body touching mine. There were lice on him, which I feared would come onto me. But they came toward me, then turned back and stayed on him! He said to me, "I educated my lice. They will never leave me."
>
> I asked his name. "Dervish Muhammad," he said. And he told me that he had sat with me nineteen years ago, on my first Pilgrimage, and remembered my fancy blue coat. He had not addressed me then on account of my youth.

On Dervish Mehmet's orders, Shaikh Nur al-'Arabi went into seclusion many times. On one occasion, while awake, he saw the Messenger of Allah (peace and blessings upon him), who bestowed upon him the levels of being "lost in Allah" and of being "existent in Allah."

When he returned to Skopia the new governor of the city, Selim Pasha, became his dervish. Selim wanted to build him his own school, but the shaikh preferred that a ruined church be repaired for him. It came to be known as Voyvoda Mosque. Selim Pasha was later called to Istanbul and promoted to the post of general of the palace guard. He then invited the shaikh to Istanbul, where Nur al-'Arabi stayed six months, meeting all the spiritual and religious leaders of the capital.

When he returned, many government and military dignitaries became his dervishes. He appeared to attract them more than he attracted the common people. He knew well that the common people would follow the influential members of society.

In 1852-3/1269 H, the Turco-Russian War began. The shaikh was invited to Manastir (now Bitolj in Yugoslavia) by General Isma'il Pasha the Circassian. There he interpreted the *Waridat* of Shaikh Badruddin to a huge crowd of intellectuals and influential people. (Most of those interpretations are included in this book.)

Because of the war with Russia, the controversial reputation of Shaikh Badruddin as a Malami revolutionary became a sensitive issue. Shaikh Nur al-'Arabi was reported to Sultan 'Abdul-'Aziz, who ordered an investigation. The shaikh's contacts in high places assured the sultan of the falseness of the accusations. Nevertheless, for his protection, the shaikh was invited to Istanbul.

And so Shaikh Nur al-'Arabi returned to Istanbul. From there he traveled, staying at the palaces of high officials. Wherever he went, not only military and government dignitaries but theologians and shaikhs of other Sufi orders attached themselves to him. During one of these trips in 1871-2/1288 H, he declared that he had been given the position of the *qutb*, the Pole of the Age. By 1874/1291 H, most of the other Sufi orders of the European regions and many in Istanbul had become his followers.

The shaikh performed the Pilgrimage many times. During the last one, in 1885/1302 H, while sitting by the well of Zamzam in Mecca, he had two dreams. In one dream the Messenger of Allah (peace and blessings upon him) showed him how to make his ritual ablution and with his own hands thrice sprinkled water over the shaikh's head. In the second the shaikh saw himself turn into Hadrat 'Ali (the nephew and son-in-law of the Prophet, called by him "the gate of the City of Knowledge"), while the Prophet (peace and blessings of Allah be upon him) told him, "You are a member of my household."

After establishing Malamiyyah anew, especially among the influential classes of the Ottoman Empire, Shaikh Nur al-'Arabi died in 1887-8/1305 H at the age of seventy-seven. He was buried in his room in Usturumja (now in Yugoslavia). He left fifty-five books—seventeen in Arabic and thirty-eight in Turkish. He was influenced particularly by Hadrat Muhyiddin Ibn 'Arabi (1165-1240/560-638 H), and Hadrat Niyazi Misri (1618-1694/1027-1105 H), as well as Shaikh Badruddin of Simawna. Some of his followers still follow his practice.

In the system of Shaikh Muhammad Nur al-'Arabi, as in all Malami systems, there are no centers, ceremonies of initiation, rituals of remembrance, particular prayers or litanies, robes, or insignia.

Malamis are not excessive in their worship and are satisfied with the obligatory and traditional prayers. Consequently, Shaikh Nur al-'Arabi's teaching acted not so much through recitation and worship as through three obligations imposed on the novice.

The first was continuous resistance to the desires of the ego. The second was continuous effort to be conscious through remembrance of Allah. The third was continuous striving to receive the secret of the unity of creation and the Creator, by eliminating the veil of duality caused by consciousness of self.

The shaikh would meet a novice in a private house and advise him in "a manner and language corresponding to the level of understanding of the dervish."

If the novice was on the level of aspiration to unity of action—that is, to the understanding of himself and the world, the understanding of witnessed events—he was asked to keep constantly on his tongue, in his mind, and in his heart the phrase *la fa'ila illa Llah*, "there is nothing that acts but Allah."

That practice might lead to the second level, aspiration to unity of attributes. At this stage the shaikh would guide the student towards the realization that all qualitative characteristics—such as living, knowing, willing, seeing, hearing, saying—point toward and become one with the Truth.

At that juncture the third level, aspiration to the unity of essence, might become possible. Here, one could be drawn to know directly that the only being is the True Being. The creation, of which man is a part, has no independent being; nor does it really exist. Visible existence is but a minute part of the manifestation of the Creator—not Him, but from Him.

With these three steps the dervish first loses his actions in the action of the One, then his character and individuality in the character of the One, and then, indeed, his very existence in the existence of the One.

Thus there is nothing to which to relate oneself—neither act, nor character, nor existence. One is not; that is the level of *la mawjuda illa Llah*. At that level, there is the joy of total independence. There is no further responsibility. All will is Allah's, and all that happens is His doing.

This Malami goal, misunderstood and misapplied by those unsuited for it, could easily lead to chaos—for many people, deceived or self-deceiving, are happy to believe that they are at the highest level, and that for them, there is no wrong and no right. Such an illusion makes for spiritual and social disaster.

This potential, a distortion of true Malamiyyah, resulted in bloody persecutions of Malamis by the rulers of earlier times. Sayyid Muhammad Nur al-'Arabi foresaw this possible degeneration and explicitly reestablished as a second foundation of Malamiyyah the discipline of following the character and behavior of the Prophet Muhammad (peace and blessings upon him)—for he was the one who knew best that indeed all will is Allah's but is manifest in those people who fear and love Allah.

Such people say:

> O seeker, do not take the wrong road, seeking Allah in time and place, with a desire of this world or the Garden of the Hereafter in your heart. Rather seek Him in your heart, for that is the place closest to Allah. The heart of the faithful is His domain. That heart is a trust within man, made from the Divine light.
>
> O seeker, know that the path to Truth is within you. You are the traveler. Going happens by itself. Coming happens to you, without you. To know is the Truth. To find is to see Him. To be is to be united with Him. There is no arriving nor leaving; nor is there any place; nor is there a contained within a container. Who is there to be with Him? What is there other than He? Who seeks and finds and is with Him when there is none but He?
>
> O enterer of the path of Malamiyyah, you with the heart's wish to be filled with the truth of love, when your heart is at peace, filled with Divine love, try to protect it. The way to protect it is by following the example of the Beloved of Allah. Like him, realize in yourself the Divine names and attributes that your Lord placed in Adam. If you do this, the darkness of your ego will leave your

heart for good, and the light of faith will shine within it.

O seeker of truth, hold the hand of a perfect shaikh who knows what is visible and invisible and the secret of Divine secrets. They are the physicians of faith, who will cure you of your arrogance by showing you where you came from and where you are going. They will reinforce you in your battle against the microbe of your ego, save you from the lusts and desires of your flesh. Do not look down on the men of religion, who teach you the rules and rituals of your religion. The fundamental obligations of your faith are the body of your being, and the mystic path is its soul. The soul without the body is a ghost, and the body without the soul is a corpse. Strengthen your body with your religion and let the mystic path cure your spiritual ills, so that you will be strong in body and soul. For you need strength to know, to find, and to be. . . .

Inspirations

CHAPTER I

Bismillah ir-Rahman ir-Rahim
In the Name of Allah, the Beneficent, the Merciful

The Divine Verse

The Divine Name *Allah* in the opening verse of the Holy Qur'an, qualified by the attributes of the Most Beneficent and the Most Merciful, is the manifestation of the Divine action that includes all and everything that happens, from before the beginning of time until after its end.

If man—the supreme creation of Allah, whom He created in His own image and into whom He breathed His own Soul as a soul—is conscious that all that happens to him, through him, and around him has nothing to do with him, and that none other than Allah the Beneficent and Merciful is the real actor, then he is the recipient of the manifestation of Allah's action. Thus man becomes the mirror and the eye that sees the Divine happening in the mirror, while he himself is excluded.

This consciousness is the beginning of the path of truth. When the novice is able to say, "*Bismillah ir-Rahman ir-Rahim*," when he comes or goes, eats or drinks, speaks or writes or thinks, then all he does is in the Name of Allah, the Beneficent and Merciful.

Deeper in the meaning of this Divine verse is the manifestation of Allah's attributes. In all that happens there is a hand, a power that causes the action that moves a thing. There is a place where each happening starts and a place where it ends. There is a time during which an action lasts and each action starts another action in turn. All this appears to be done by things, to things.

These actions and their effects have qualities: short or long, slow or fast, constructive or destructive, beautiful or ugly, right or wrong. All these and infinitely more quantitative and qualitative characteristics of all existence, including ourselves, are the manifestations of Allah's attributes and are the proof of His existence and reality.

When we are able to see these characteristics of existence around us and within us without considering ourselves to be causing or possessing any of them, when we can attribute them all to the Creator, then we become recipients of the manifestation of Allah's attributes.

Still deeper in the secret of this Divine verse is hidden the manifestation of Allah's essence. The one who penetrates this secret will see that man is not only unable to do (for Allah is the sole Doer) and unable to possess anything, even his own personality (for all belongs to Allah)—but that man does not even exist—the only existence is Him. This person will be the recipient of the manifestation of Allah's essence.

> Between the Two Worlds my Lord a city built.
> If you can see, you see Him all around it.
> I found myself there and saw it being built.
> Put between the stones I was built into it.
>
> Hajji Bayram Wali

The city built by the Lord is humanity; that city has four gates. The first gate is the manifestation of the Lord's action, through which He sees the conscious one who sees Him. The second gate of the city is the gate of the manifestation of the Lord's attributes. He sees His own attributes reflected in all beings. The third gate is the gate of the Lord's beautiful names, and He sees through that gate His names manifested in His creation. The fourth gate is the gate of the manifestation of His essence, through which He views Himself.

If the seer and the seen become one when the Divine phrase "In the Name of Allah the Beneficent, the Merciful" is pronounced, then the act and the actor and the action are all Truth. If the words are just pronounced—without any consciousness of whose act the action is and who the real doer is, and that all and everything is united and one—then that which is pronounced is merely sound.

Divine manifestations are through the Divine decree and have nothing to do with words. The novice needs to give the Divine decree a form in words, but the unified one, who is not divided into a thousand "I"s within himself, has no need of words. When a good act is manifested through him, he is in a state of unity (*jam'*) with the True Actor. He does not attribute the good deed to himself, but is thankful that he was chosen as a good channel. When a maleficent action appears through him, he is in a state of separation (*farq*). He attributes the wrong to himself, although he is still in union with his Lord, in obedience to His words:

> ... whatever good happens to you, it is from Allah.
> Whatever bad happens to you, it is from yourself. ...
>
> (Nisa', 4:79)

The secret meaning of the essential verse of the Holy Qur'an—*Bismillah ir-Rahman ir-Rahim*—is hidden within the first letter of the phrase, within the point under the Arabic letter "*B*" (ب). All Divine secrets are contained within this dot.

Some of the Companions asked Hadrat 'Ali (may Allah be pleased with him), "O 'Ali, the Messenger of Allah (may Allah's peace and blessings be upon him), said about you, 'I am the city of knowledge and 'Ali is its gate.' What did he mean by that?"

Hadrat 'Ali (may Allah be pleased with him) answered, "All Divine

The Divine Verse

knowledge is within the books sent to the one hundred and twenty-four thousand prophets since Adam (upon him be peace). All the Divine knowledge within these books is within the Holy Qur'an, the last book sent to the last prophet and the Seal of Prophethood, Muhammad (may Allah's peace and blessings be upon him). All that is in the Holy Qur'an is in the meaning of the opening chapter, the Fatihah:

> *Bismillah ir-Rahman ir-Rahim*
> *al-hamdu li-Llahi Rabbil-'alamin*
> *ar-Rahman ir-Rahim*
> *Maliki yawm id-din*
> *Iyyaka na'budu wa iyyaka nasta'in*
> *ihdinas-sirat al-mustaqim*
> *sirat alladhina an'amta 'alayhim*
> *ghayril-maghdubi 'alayhim wa lad-dalin.*

In the Name of Allah, the Beneficent,
    The Merciful.
Praise be to Allah, the Lord of the worlds,
The Beneficent, the Merciful,
Master of the Day of Requital.
Thee do we serve and
    Thee do we beseech for help.
Guide us on the right path,
The path of those upon whom
    Thou hast bestowed favors,
Not those upon whom wrath is brought down,
    nor those who go astray.

"That which is in the Fatihah is within its first verse. That which is within its first verse is within the letter "*B*." That which is within all and everything is in the point under the letter "*B*" (ب). I am that point."

The Companions asked, "O intimate of Allah, how could all that fit into a dot?"

Hadrat 'Ali (may Allah be pleased with him) answered, "*al-'ilmu nuktah. Kasarahul-jahilun*" (Knowledge is but a point. It is the ignorant who increased it).

When the pen touches the paper, before it moves and writes a book, it first produces a dot. That point is the beginning and the essence of all the letters and words within the book. It contains them all.

A place is entered through a door. Once one has passed through the door, one is in that space. This is a secret. If the mind understood it, it could stop thinking further. This small inspired work is like that dot, and what it contains, the heavens could not contain.

Bismillah ir-Rahman ir-Rahim is the origin.

All existence, seen and unseen, originates from the three Divine Names within this essential verse: *Allah; Rahman,* the All-Beneficent; and *Rahim,* the All-Merciful.

Within existence there is bad as well as good. There are scorpions, snakes, beasts, disasters, pain, sickness, the Devil, evil. All these and other things like them are the manifestation of Allah's attribute *Jalal,* the Almighty, which appears as a crushing force upon the universe.

All existence is made in a perfect balance of good and evil, pleasure and pain, comfort and difficulty. This balance of seemingly opposing qualities is the manifestation of Allah's Name, *Rahman,* the All-Beneficent, which contains both Allah's might and wrath and His grace and kindness in perfect balance, one complementing the other.

Because of the perfection of this balance, *Rahman,* the All-Beneficent, is also called the Name of Perfection. This Beneficence is to be experienced in this life, within this world, where sweet is not understood without bitter, joy without sadness, light without darkness.

The Divine Verse

The Beautiful Name of Allah *Rahim*, the All-Merciful, contains only Allah's grace and kindness.

In a Divine precept Allah, addressing man, says, "I created all for you, and I created you for Myself." All that Allah has created for man is the expression of His Divine Name *Rahman*, Beneficent. When He says He created man for Himself, it is the expression of His beautiful Name *Rahim*, His mercy in the Hereafter.

Allah the Creator exists eternally from before the before to after the after. All the universes of matter and the forces within them are the manifestation of His attribute *Rahman*, the Beneficent. All that is contained in the Hereafter is a manifestation of His name *Rahim*, the All-Merciful. Together they are the whole of existence.

Allah has created man as His deputy, the connection between Him and His creation. He declared this to His angels:

*wa idh qala rabbuka lil-mala'ikati
inni ja'ilun fil-ardi khalifah*

When the Lord said to the angels,
I am going to place a deputy in the earth. . . .

(Baqarah, 2:30)

Man is honored with this state because the Lord taught him His Divine Names. When He had done so, He asked Hadrat Adam (upon him be peace) his own name. Adam responded, "I do not know. I have none." Then the Lord said, "For this I make you My deputy to rule the worlds."

This is the secret of the sacred verse *Bismillah ir-Rahman ir-Rahim*. When pronouncing it, if one forgets himself, excludes himself, then what one does is done by Allah.

That which connects the visible worlds to the invisible Hereafter is he whom Allah sent as His "mercy upon the universe." His mercy, which belongs to the Hereafter, came among us into the world of matter, appearing as a man like us:

*laqad ja'akum rasulun min anfusikum 'azizun 'alayhi
ma 'anittum
harisun 'alaykum bil-mu'minina ra'ufun rahim.*

Certainly a Messenger has come to you from among yourselves. Grievous to him is your falling into error, most anxious is he for you; to the believers (he is) compassionate and merciful.

(Tawbah, 9:28)

Through him He has sent the essence of all and everything: *Bismillah ir-Rahman ir-Rahim.* He is Muhammad Mustafa (may Allah's peace and blessings be upon him), the last and Seal of Prophets, the light of whose soul is the first creation of Allah. May Allah's peace and blessings be upon his soul and upon the souls of the people of his house and upon his companions and people. *Amin.*

CHAPTER II

The Hereafter

> Know that the affairs of the next world
> are not what the ignorant claim. . . .

What happens beyond the grave is not what some claim and some believe. Things are not the way they are described by those who misunderstand: tortures, chains, scorpions, snakes, demons for the sinners; rose gardens lighted by many moons, angel companions, rivers of honey and wine, palaces, and virgins transparent as crystals for the pure blameless ones.

What happens in the Hereafter belongs to the realm of the spirit. It is not of this world of matter; nor can it bear any resemblance to anything material. This world of matter consists of bodies— of mineral, vegetable, and animal existences that appear, grow and die, that are built and destroyed, that move and change, which have three dimensions within a limited space and time. All that is within this world ends, and just as it did not exist in time immemorial, at some point it will all disappear. The only thing in the world that will go to the Hereafter and will not disappear is the *ruh*, the soul—which does not even belong to the world.

The matters of the Hereafter are known to Allah alone. They concern the fine matter of spirit, which resembles nothing here:

wa yas'alunaka 'an ir-ruhi. Qul ir-ruhu min amri rabbi.

And they ask you about the soul. Say that it is (only) in the knowledge of my Lord and in His decree.

(Isra', 17:5)

The soul belongs to the *'alam al-ghayb*, the world of absence, invisible to our material eyes in the sense that it does not contain anything that is experienced in this world. Allah's spiritual kingdom is spaceless and timeless. Not even the ones closest to Allah, His intimates, know it. Hadrat 'Ali (may Allah be pleased with him) said, *"law kashsafal-ghita'i ma izdadtu yaqinan"* (Even if my veils were lifted, my certainty would not increase).

Even if the experiences, the concepts, all the knowledge of this world and of this life—as well as words and images as reference, as association, as comparison—would disappear (for all these are nothing but veils), one could not understand nor see that which is beyond. Yet the soul sees and knows.

Abu Talib al-Makki described the soul:

> When the spirit of the believer is freed from the body of matter at death, it knows its Lord with the knowledge of its Lord because it has not forgotten its origin, because it remembered and yearned while it was in the prison of the living body. It rises to return to Him. There is no resistance in its flight; neither air nor gravity slow it down. There is no difficulty, or anything unknown to it. It rises to where it is destined and takes the form of its worldly appearance, transformed to an image of fine matter according to the imagery of the realm in which it is destined to reside.

The soul's image is beautified to the extent of the purity, piety, and good deeds it achieved during its worldly existence, and the name of the high realm reached by the souls of the faithful is *Illiyin*. Its distance is beyond the human heavens, ranging from the moon to the Footstool of Allah, which is the base of Divine knowledge, power, and dominion. That is where the eight gardens of Paradise are situated, as mentioned in the Holy Qur'an:

> *innal-muttaqina fi jannatin wa naharin fi maq'adi sidqin 'inda malikim-muqtadir.*
>
> Surely the dutiful will be among (eight) gardens and rivers, in the seat of truth with a most Powerful King.
>
> (Qamar, 54:54-55)

The eight gardens of Paradise are:

the gardens of *waliyyah*—sainthood, where those who were loyal to the truth of Allah reside;

the gardens of *siddiqiyyah*—righteousness, the gardens where the sincere and the truthful reside;

the gardens of *qurbiyyah*—closeness, where the intimates of Allah, those who are close to Him, reside;

the gardens of *khullah*—friendship, where the pure reside;

the gardens of *mahabbah*—love, where His lovers reside;

the gardens of *khitam*—completion, where the unified, completed perfect souls reside;

the gardens of *'ubudah*—devotion, where those who are in the service of Allah reside;

The gardens of *'ubudiyyah*—servanthood, where the loving slaves in the bondage of Allah reside.

Inspirations

If the soul belongs to a sinner, when it leaves the body it also has no form or shape; yet it is heavy, not with material but with conceptual weight. It descends in accordance with its weight until it sinks to the lowest of the low—*asfal as-safilin*. The seven hells mentioned in the Holy Qur'an are in these realms.

The souls of sinners assume the character of their animal selves. If, in this world, one was insatiately ambitious, one's soul assumes the character of a pig. If one was arrogant, thinking that one is great and that others are lowly, it will assume the character of an elephant. If one was envious and jealous, one will assume the character of a monkey. Each character of different weight will sink in accordance with the weight of its sin.

Some think that the Hereafter is like the world of matter because Allah Most High addresses man in the language of man. They think in terms of what the word calls to mind, which is material, while the reality is the word itself, which is of the essence, immaterial, conceptual. They base their contention on verses such as:

Qul yuhiyha alladhi ansha'aha awwala marratin wa huwa 'ala kulli khalqin 'alim.

Say: He Who brought them into existence at first, will give life to them and He is knower of all creation.

(Ya Sin, 36:79)

a wa laysa lladhi khalaqas-samawati wal-arda bi-qadirin 'ala 'an yakhluqa mithlahum? Bala, wa huwal-khallaq ul-'alim.

Is not He Who created the heavens and the earth able to create the like of them? Yea, and He is the Creator, the Knower.

(Ya Sin, 36:81)

Although in this verse Allah says He is able to create the *like* of them, they claim that He will create them the same. They say that there is a tiny piece of bone at the end of one's spinal column that does not rot, and that on the Day of Judgment, like corn from planted grain, man will grow from this remnant to be just as he was in the world.

If we must seek something existing now that will be the same in the Hereafter, it is certainly not material form, shape, or body. Perhaps it is the word—if one knew what one was saying; if it were not just noise—for the true word is produced by the soul.

The body changes and ages; not a single cell remains in one's body that was there twenty years ago. Yet the essence, the soul, is the same, whether one is a baby or an old man. It is that which will be returning to its Lord. It is that which will appear on the Day of Judgment and go to Paradise or Hell. Otherwise, if someone lost his hand or foot while he was a child and then was thrown into hellfire for his sins later in life, would it be just for the blameless hand or foot to burn? For Allah says:

> *fa-man ya'malu mithqala dharratin khayran yarah,*
> *wa man ya'malu mithqala dharratin sharran yarah.*
>
> So he who does an atom's weight of good will see it, and he who does an atom's weight of evil will see it.
>
> (Zilzal, 99:7-8)

The Prophet (may Allah's peace and blessings be upon him) said, "*inna ma hiya a'malukum raddat 'alaykum*" (Your deeds, whether good or bad, will be returned to you).

At the time of the *mi'raj*, the ascension of the Prophet (may Allah's peace and blessings be upon him) to the realms beyond, Hadrat Ibrahim (upon him be peace) told him, "O Muhammad (may Allah's peace and blessings be upon him), tell your people that Paradise is void. There are neither trees nor rivers nor palaces within. The gardens of Paradise, the blessings therein, are the words, *subhan Allahi wal-hamdu li-Llahi wa la ilaha illa Llahu wa Llahu akbar* (Exalted is Allah, praise is Allah's; there is no god but Allah: Allah is greater). Tell them to repeat these words often."

The existences beyond life—after death, in the tomb, in Purgatory, on the day of Last Judgment, in Hell and Paradise—are neither of this world nor resemble anything in this world. One will be recreated in the shape of one's *sirr*, one's essence, and the realm within which one will find oneself will be the realm of concepts, of the meaning of one's life and actions in this world.

Allah says:

yawma tublas-sara'ir. . . .

On the day when hidden things are manifested. . . .

(Tariq, 86:9)

That day is the life beyond, and the "hidden things" are the essences of things. This world is nothing but an illusion—a dream, not reality. How could the actual reality of the Hereafter be the recreation of an illusion or have any resemblance to it?

The Prophet (may Allah's peace and blessings be upon him) said, "*an-nasu yanamu wa idha matu intabihu.*" (Men are asleep. They wake up only when they die.)

Thus the only way man can know what is beyond life is by following the order of the Messenger of Allah (may Allah's peace and blessings be upon him), who said, "*mutu qabla an tamutu*" (Die before you die) so that you can see the true reality of your eternal self and the reality of eternity.

CHAPTER III

On the Limitations of Physical Existence

The body is a compound of elements, and every compound is created and will pass away.

The physical body that we call the human being belongs to the realm of the chemical elements of this world. That is what we glorify as humanity. Humanity as it exists in this life cannot be that which will return to its Lord because humanity depends on its physical existence. It depends on the body.

The body is a compound made of chemical elements. Every compound is a new thing that has come into existence, a thing that did not exist before, and in time it must decompose and cease to exist. The elements of which the body is composed cannot be reformed into their past form. Even if it were possible to recompose the body into its original shape, it would be bound to decompose again.

These chemical elements are simple matter. They cannot become compound by themselves.

All of nature and all of the things produced from nature are compounds made of the same chemical elements. In their decomposition they return to their origin, to the principal elements of fire, water, earth, and air. The elements from which the human body is composed are refinements of these four principal elements.

These elements as they are combined in every cell did not exist before the compound existence that we call the body.

It is certain that all matter that exists in the composition of the body, after its decomposition, cannot be recomposed to its original form. It is also certain that these elements will return to their original source of fire, water, earth, and air. At the end, finally, even water, earth, and air will return to their origin, which is fire. The end of all that is material is fire. That is what is called "Hell."

If the human being is his body, a body composed of matter has no place in heaven, for all that is in heaven is eternal. Heaven cannot accept a compound, which is bound to decompose. All physical existence is bound to return to its origin, which is fire, and finally all that will exist of matter is fire. The only bodies that will be saved from fire are the ones whom Allah addresses in a divine tradition:

Arwahukum, ashbahukum. Ashbahukum, arwahukum.

Your souls will be your bodies and your bodies will be your souls.

These are the bodies of Allah's faithful servants who reach that high state because they understand and obey His reason for creating them, when He said:

kuntu kanzan makhfiyan fa-ahbabtu an u'rafa fa khalaqtul-khalqa li-u'raf.

I was a hidden treasure, I yearned to be known, so I created creation.

When He said, "*fa-ahbabtu an u'rafa*" (I yearned to be known), His yearning to be known is because of His love for the ones who know Him. These are the ones whose bodies He transforms into

On the Limitations of Physical Existence

spirit, and whose souls He transforms into bodies, and whose souls and bodies become one and the same. As the physical bodies of those beloved of Allah many appear in an ethereal shape in this life, so in the Hereafter the souls will have their own shape in the imagery of the life beyond.

In this life and in this world of matter and phenomena there is already an example of a reality other than that which we see ordinarily, a visionary world that coexists with the visible world. It has two facets. The first is visions that are limited, a world we visit in dreams. In this world concepts, ideas, and meanings assume form and shape, which we call symbols. For ordinary people the meaning of these visions must be interpreted according to the imagery and language of ordinary life. For the prophets, the saints, and the ones close to Allah these dreams need not be interpreted. Their being is such that they inhabit both the visible world and the world of visions. Therefore, what they see in one world is not different from what they see in the other.

The other facet of the visionary world is not dependent on dreams. It is as concrete as the visible world. In that world the images of fine matter are concentrated to appear as do the images of coarse matter in this world; yet they seem more ethereal, as if light were shining through them like an image reflected in a mirror. When the archangel Gabriel (upon him be peace) came to the Prophet (may Allah's peace and blessings be upon him) bringing Allah's revelations, he appeared as a beautiful man.

For those who are conscious of the reality of their souls, both the experiences of this world and the visions of what is beyond are shadows, illusions, and nothing more.

***

All that exists is to be found in each thing; indeed, in every atom. . . .

In all that is seen, in all that is experienced, are the manifestations of Allah's attributes, for that is the meaning of existence, the purpose of its creation and of Allah's intention. That is the meaning of the Lord Who owns and controls all, and is everywhere. The whole is in the all. All existence is within every existence. All existence is within every atom. This is the beautiful image of Allah, of His names, and of His attributes, which we see as multiplicity, while Allah's intent is to show Himself in His Unity, His Oneness.

All that exists within the whole created universe, even within the uncreated Divinity Himself, is hidden within each atom—all except the essence of Allah. The whole universe is within the atom; thus the whole is within the smallest particle of what we see as multiplicity. The totality of existence is but a part of the atom in an intrinsic sense, though in an evident external sense, the atom appears to be a part of existence. That is how the universe is structured.

This unifying force is the cause of all existence. This cause is Allah's essence, while existence itself is only the manifestation of Allah's attributes.

Allah's essence in Its uniqueness is free from any resemblance to anything else. It is by Itself and known only to Itself. It cannot even be described as all and everything, or as the one and only thing. But Allah's attributes are manifested as the reality in all and everything in the universe, and the whole is within the smallest element in the making of the whole.

All the energy and power within everything is locked in its smallest particle; in every atom the divine power is hidden. Yet the whole is not visible, for the fire is hidden within the flint, and within the seed is the entire tree. As the seed grows, the huge trunk and branches, and the thousands of leaves and flowers that were hidden in it, appear.

All creation is a visible proof of the Creator. All creative energy is within every atom of the creation, and every atom contains the whole creative potential, lacking nothing. All existence, in its essential nature, appears in the atom. All the secrets of the universe are in it, in all aspects, even the hidden aspects. Yet these inner spiritual aspects of existence, though part of the smallest particle of matter, are not material themselves.

CHAPTER IV

On the Revelation of Mysteries to the Knowers of Allah

In reality there is no such thing as an invisible world. The invisible realms mentioned in the holy books are only invisible in relation to man who is part blind. For the Truth there is nothing unseen, hidden, or secret.

There are three levels of looking into what we call the unseen. The lowest level is a kind of intuitive God-given sight, like the kind mentioned in the saying of the Prophet (may Allah's peace and blessings be upon him):

ittaqu firasat il-mu'min, fa-innahu yanzuru bi-nuri Llah.

Beware of the sight of the faithful who sees beyond appearances, because he sees with the light of Allah.

This kind of sight is strengthened with the awareness of the presence of Allah, which brings one to an ecstatic consciousness.

The second kind of deeper perception is seeing through symbols, in which finer matter is transformed into coarser matter. An example is the appearance of the archangel Gabriel (upon him be peace) to the Prophet (may Allah's peace and blessings be upon him) as a beautiful man, or the appearance of the angel of death, Azrael (upon him be peace), who one day sat among the Companions as a man and announced to the Prophet (may Allah's peace and blessings be upon him) that one of them had only an hour to live. When the man asked, "O Messenger of Allah, what should I do with this one hour of life?" the Source of Wisdom responded, "Learn ... so that you may see more of that which is beyond, as you have seen the one who has come to take your soul."

The ability to see beyond this world comes through this kind of symbolic vision. With it, neither does the view of this world become a veil for that which is beyond, nor does the perception of the beyond become a veil to the view of this world.

The highest form of revelation of the beyond to the knowers of Allah comes as a clear manifestation beyond what is here and now, as clearly seen as something right in front of one. An example of this was when Hadrat 'Umar (may Allah be pleased with him), while preaching in the mosque in Medina, was shown the battle on the plain of Nihawand in Persia. He shouted to the commander of the Muslim armies, "O Sariya, to the mountain, to the mountain!" and Sariya heard his voice from several months' distance.

Allah Most High says in a divine revelation:

kuntu kanzan makhfiyan fa-ahbabtu an u'rafa fa-khalaqtal-khalqa li-u'raf.

I was a hidden treasure (a pure essence, absolute existence clear of all existence, image or likeness), I loved to be known, so I created the creation (when all and everything became a reflection of My attributes, the symbols of My Essence) so that it might know Me.

Allah's Essence is neither seen nor unseen. It is neither outer nor inner, known only to Himself. All there is in the creation—

which is not Him, but is from Him—is a manifestation of His knowledge of Himself, a reflection of the divine Idea. Before the creation there was nothing but Him. After the creation there is nothing but Him. The Prophet (may Allah's peace and blessings be upon him) said:

kana Llahu wa-lam yakun ma'ahu shay'un, wa huw-alan 'ala ma 'alayhi kan.

Allah existed and nothing else existed with Him, and now Allah exists and nothing else exists with Him.

"I loved to be known, so I created the creation" is reflected in the ones whom Allah loves among His creation. Within His creation, the attributes indicating His perfection are reflected only in man. The qualities of living, knowing, hearing, seeing, will, power, talking, and the dependence of all else are His gifts to humanity. But his greatest gift is love, the manifestation of His love of knowing Himself. Love is the primary sustenance for human beings. They cannot live without it, and mankind learned to love from Allah.

Love is given to man so that he may seek and find the Beloved. It is that which creates energy in the creation, an energy produced by the inclination of the Divine will to be known that is reflected upon man. The love of man for Allah and his love for his own kind and for all else that he loves is the name of this energy. All creation, all that has happened and is happening, comes about through love.

Allah created the creation so that the creation would know Him, and love is the means both of creation and of knowing Him, and to know Him is the purpose of love. Whenever love has for a goal anything other than knowing Him, the life-giving energy in it escapes, and love is lost.

On the Revelations of the Mysteries

Allahumm-arzuqna hadhihil-mahabbah.

O Lord, bless us with the life-giving sustenance of this love.

***

There is no existence other than Allah, and the knowledge of Him and the knower of Him are not other than He. There is no possibility of a being other than the Being of the Absolute Truth. The Truth assumes the appearance of known truths, then is reflected upon the ones who know these truths. So the knowers of the Truth appear as existences through the reflection of the Truth upon them. In this process there is neither the penetration of the knowledge into the knower nor a union of the two, because one thing entering into another or things uniting with each other presumes the existence of two things, such as water penetrating into plants or cream within milk. There is only one divine truth. Although Allah possesses and contains everything and His attributes are the identity, the reality, the truth of His creation, Allah in His Uniqueness is devoid of all associations.

***

If the bright flame of the wick of a lamp delights the eye, what a burst of light will be the enlightened heart illuminated with a thousand torches!

The place where the Truth is manifested is the heart of the believer. The "delight of the eye" (*safa*) is the peace and certainty of the clear vision of truth that eliminates the fear of the darkness of ignorance. The "wick in flame" (*sina*) is the heart where the secret truth becomes manifest. Mount Sinai is called *tur al-sina* because that is where the secret of the Truth fell upon the heart of Moses (upon him be peace). Allah Most High says:

Allahu nur us-samawati wal-ard. Mathalu nurihi ka-mishqatin fiha misbah. Al-misbahu fi-zujajat. Az-zujajatu ka-annaha kawkabun dhurriyun yu'qadu min shajaratin mubarakatin zaytunatin la sharqiyatin wa la gharbiyah. Zaytuha yudiya'u wa law lam tamsas-hu nar. Nurun 'ala nur.

Allah is the light of the heavens and the earth. A likeness of His light is as a niche in which is a lamp—the lamp is in a glass, the glass is as it were a bright shining star—lit from a blessed olive tree neither eastern nor western, the oil whereof gives light, though fire touches it not—light upon light. . . .

(Nur, 24:39)

Nur, the divine light, is that which manifests the secret truth. *Mishqat*, the niche, is the visible material universe. *Zujaj*, the glass, which is "as it were a bright shining star," is the spirit. The oil which gives light "though fire touches it not" is Allah's attributes and beautiful names manifest in the creation. *Shajarah*, the blessed tree neither of the east nor of the west, is Divine knowledge. *Misbah*, the lamp, is Allah's existence. The Divine verse shows the Truth manifested in Allah's Being, in His divine knowledge, in His beautiful names and attributes, in the spirit, and in the visible material universe. These are called His "five exalted Presences" which are entrusted to mankind.

Allah has left His trust to humanity for safekeeping.

inna 'aradna al-amanata 'alas-samawati wal-ardi wal-jibali fa-abayna an tahmilnaha wa ashfaqna minha wa hamalaha al-insan. Innahu kana zuluman jahula.

> We did indeed offer the Trust to the heavens and the earth and the mountains, but they refused to undertake it, being afraid thereof, but man undertook it. He was indeed unjust and ignorant.
>
> (Ahzab, 33:72)

Those who know the truth say that the Trust comprises the materialization of the Truth, and that Adam was created in this form. This is to be found in the human being, not in anything else.

The trust that Allah asked His creation to bear is the knowledge of Him. It is the Truth, and man himself is created in the image of Truth, and the Truth is only fully manifest in man, not in anything else created. Therefore nothing else in the whole creation is worthy to bear Allah's trust. The material composition of other creations is inappropriate to carry such a load; yet man, even in his material being, accepted to carry Allah's trust. His injustice and ignorance refer only to his material being, not to that which is divine in him. He evolved into a just and wise being only through the mercy of Allah that descended upon him when he accepted His trust.

When Allah addresses Himself as "We," He expresses His aspect that gathers together all truth and contains all His creation. When He says "the trust," He means the secret of the power to rule given to man as His deputy on earth. For He said

> ... lil-mala'ikati inni ja'ilun fil-ardi khalifah.
>
> ... to the angels, I am going to place a deputy to rule in the earth.
>
> (Baqarah, 2:30)

This is the secret that even His angels did not know, and that secret was first given to Hadrat Muhammad Mustafa (may Allah's peace and blessings be upon him), whose light, whose soul, whose wisdom was the first creation. That trust is the beautiful names of Allah which

... 'allama Adam. ...

... He taught Adam. ...

(Baqarah, 2:31)

In the divine verse on the Trust, what is meant by "the heavens" is the higher realms. What is meant by "the earth" is the lower worlds. What is meant by "the mountains" is all the creations that the higher heavens and the lower worlds contain, all of which lack the aptitude in their nature to bear the Divine trust. They therefore declined, and their declining was their begging for Allah's compassion. In cognizance of their incapacity to carry the whole of the trust, Allah's compassion enabled them to carry some of His attributes.

When Allah offered to the Pen all His Beautiful Names—within which are hidden the mystery of the power to rule—His deputy, the Pen (which He created first in order to teach Him to His creation) said that it could carry only His Name *al-Badi'*, the Originator from which all else is originated.

When He proposed His trust to the Tablet where His decrees are preserved, the Tablet said that it could only bear His Name *al-Ba'ith*, the Revealer.

When He offered His trust to Nature, it only took His Name *al-Batin*, the Hidden Essence.

When He proposed His trust to material things, they could only bear His Name *al-Akhir*, the Last.

The images accepted His Name *az-Zahir*, the Manifest One.

The elemental substance took His Name *al-Hakim*, the Absolute Wisdom.

The empyrean Throne took His Name *al-Muhit*, the All-Comprehending.

His heavenly Footstool, the basis of the universe, took His Name *ash-Shakur*, the One who Rewards the Grateful.

Then He offered His trust to the heavenly spheres. The ninth sphere, the sphere of *Atlas*, took His Name *al-Ghani*, the Generous Possessor of All.

The sphere of the twenty-eight mansions of the moon accepted the Divine Name *al-Muqtadir*, the Empowering.

The planet Saturn took the Name *ar-Rabb*, the Lord Who Raises His creation to Maturity.

Jupiter took the attribute *al-'Alim*, the All-Knowing.

Mars took the attribute *al-Muhsi*, the Possessor of Quantitative Knowledge.

The moon took the attribute *al-Mubin*, the Distinguisher.

The ether accepted the Name *al-Muhyi*, the Giver of Life.

The earth took the Name *al-Mumit*, the Creator of Death.

The minerals took the Name *al-'Aziz*, the Precious One.

The vegetation took the Name *ar-Razzaq*, the Sustainer.

The animals took the Name *al-Mudhill*, the Abaser.

The angels took the Name *al-Qawi*, the Possessor of Strength.

The jinn took the Name *al-Latif*, the Graceful.

And when Allah proposed His trust to man, he took the Name *al-Jami'*, the Gatherer, the one name which unites within itself all the Divine attributes.

Man's being called "unjust and ignorant" at the end of the verse on the Trust refers to his covering and hiding the Divine attributes that he possesses, as the darkness of the night hides what it contains. For man is the keeper of Allah's trust, of the secret of being Allah's deputy, in whom all His names are manifest.

Huge mountains viewed from a distance look like dark mounds. It is not possible to distinguish all the things that exist upon these mountains. Just so, it is not possible to make out what is contained within the multiplicity. It is as if the darkness of injustice covers the multiplicity. But when one comes close to it, then one is able to see. From afar the general is seen; from nearby the particular is seen. The wise see the unity in the generality. And the wise who are able to differentiate and discriminate in the multiplicity can eliminate the differences and are entranced in union with Allah. It is said that the wise who are born at night come to know Allah in the unity within the generality, and the ones who are born in daytime come to know Him within the multiplicity of differences.

Perhaps Allah's calling man ignorant is due to man's inability to discriminate within the multiplicity. As Allah describes his state,

fa-aynama tuwallu fa-thamma wajhu Llah.

Wherever you turn, there is the presence of Allah.

(Baqarah, 2:115)

***

Not only do beings and things have spirits which in turn take the forms of beings and things, but deeds, words, thoughts, and feelings also have spirits of their own. It happens that the soul of a beautiful deed may assume the form of an angel.

In a tradition of the Prophet (may Allah's peace and blessings be upon him) it is mentioned that as many angels are created as the number of letters in prayers recited for Allah's sake or in blessings upon His Prophet. These angels repeat those prayers and offer the gift of their rewards to the people who remember Allah and pray to Him. When such souls appear in their idyllic forms they are called either angels or spirits of prayers, and they are in the service of the ones who utter Divine words in sincerity.

Therefore it is important that people whose duty it is to lead others in faith and religion should have no purpose in life except to seek the Truth. Those who wish to follow a guide must seek such sincere and devoted people and shy away from people bound to the life of this world. Indeed, the Holy Qur'an often warns us to keep apart from people who have turned away from the remembrance of Allah in favor of the pleasures of this world, and we are told not to follow the ones whose hearts are rendered heedless to the remembrance of Allah, who are the slaves of their flesh and whose affairs are in turmoil. Our Master the Messenger of Allah (may Allah's peace and blessings be upon him) says about such folk, "Whoever does not turn towards Truth while praying has not prayed."

***

inna Llahu yaf'alu ma yasha'.

Indeed, Allah carries out all that He wills.

(Hajj, 22:18)

And whoever defies His will must suffer pain and disgrace, for His will is always done,

inna Llahu yahkumu ma yurid.

. . . for Allah commands according to His will and plan.

(Ma'idah, 5:1)

Allah's will is carried out in accordance with His plan, in which is reflected His perfect wisdom and goodness. It must be understood that His will is not arbitrary. He wills and does a thing in consideration of the potential and the predisposition of that thing. Allah's will is in accordance with the predisposition of that which He wills.

Every thing, every action, takes a form and becomes apparent through the will of Allah. Certain states, and levels of these states caused by inner and outer influences, create the predisposition for the materialization of Allah's will. The effect of the Divine will, after its first manifestation, is to create a whole chain of actions necessitated by its existence. Then every happening is nothing more or less than the Divine knowledge of the predisposition of a thing that will happen. Each thing thus has its potential and possibility of becoming activated through being in harmony and accepting Allah's attribute of the Originator, the One upon Whom all existence and action depend.

There are six causes that, coming together, are combined to produce this end. Three of them are active causes; they are the doers. Three of them are passive; they have the predisposition to receive action. This is the secret of the so-called trinity. When the three active causes unite with the three possibilities of action, Allah's will becomes. Nothing can prevent its happening and its existence. Yet there is the possibility of changing the course of a happening after it occurs, not by changing the action, but by participating—by adding the manifestation of the Divine power in man to the Divine power in the action created by Allah's will.

This is how necessity should be understood. Allah is not obliged to do what He does; when the causes are present, the action takes place. Allah says:

innama qawluna li-shay'in idha aradnahu an naqulu lahu kun fa-yakun.

For to anything which We have willed We but say the word "Be," and it is.

(Nahl, 16:40)

Human beings may accept their predisposition to receive Allah's will or not. The smaller will given to mankind exists only within this possibility, and Divine praise and punishment depend on this choice. Allah's will is also manifest in the animal kingdom, but the animals are not given a choice to make.

Man must accept Allah's will; yet he also has the option of

accepting or rejecting the bad and sinful acts which may come through him. For instance, one may do things in anger which one regrets later. In anger the intelligence is lost, and so is the possibility of an intelligent choice. But in the manifestation of the Lord's will in action—whether it is the manifestation of His Beneficence or His Wrath—there is a clear choice.

***

So, know that there is an intrinsic, essential predisposition within the creation.

It becomes evident from what has been explained that what is destined to happen is dependent on Allah's wish to create a thing or to cause a situation in accordance with the predisposition and the level of the thing that is to be created or the situation that is to occur. That marks the extent of man's ability to choose.

If what happens, and what one is to become, are dependent upon what one is and what one's potential is—if that is the meaning of destiny—then there does not appear to be a way to change it. If so, what is the reason for the existence of men of wisdom and religious guides—indeed, even of prophets and Divine books?

This is what Divine will and its effect upon the creation appear to be: that the Divine will operates in relation to pre-existing causes. And such is the point of view of those whose opinions depend on what is visible. What appears to them is that both good and evil are done in accordance with the will of Allah. Indeed, it is Allah Who creates both good and evil—but Allah, sacred truth, and the Divine will are far beyond and other than that which is apparent.

Allah says:

ma asabaka min hasanatin fa-min Allahi wa ma asabaka min sayi'atin fa-min nafsik.

Whatever good happens to you, it is from Allah. Whatever bad happens to you, it is from yourself....

(Nisa', 4:79)

All is explained in the verse before this, in which Allah says:

kullun min 'indi Llah. fa-ma li-ha'ula'il-qawmu la yakaduna yafqahuna haditha.

All is from Allah, but what is the matter with these people that they make no effort to understand anything?

(Nisa', 4:78)

To understand, one must make an effort. Making the effort is man's choice. With that effort, one would understand that "all is from Allah" applies to the creation of all, but not to the understanding of the creation by the created. When good things happened to the best of the creation, Hadrat Muhammad (may Allah's peace and blessings be upon him), made himself disappear, knowing them to be from Allah, and he praised Him. When bad things happened to him, he saw them as issuing from himself, hid Allah in his heart, showed patience, and praised Him.

The creation is from Allah. The understanding befalls mankind.

Hadrat Ibn 'Abbas said that the Prophet (may Allah's peace and blessings be upon him) said:

Allah created a hundred thousand Adams before Adam (upon him be peace).

Hadrat Muhyiddin ibn 'Arabi related:

One night I was circumambulating the Ka'bah.

On the Revelations of the Mysteries

I heard a spirit tell me, "Like you we have turned around this divine house in great numbers and in great joy so many years ago!"

"Whose spirit are you?" I asked.

"I am your ancestor," said the spirit.

"When did you leave this world?" I asked.

He said, "A hundred and twenty thousand years ago."

I said, "Adam was not created then."

The spirit said, "Which Adam? The one who is close to you in time, or the one further in time? I am of the progeny of the Adam who is further in time."

The Greatest of Shaikhs said that the Lord created the universe like a corpse without spirit and that He created Adam as the spirit of the universe. With the spirit, the body becomes cognizant of itself and the One Who created it. That is the perfect man.

The Prophet (may Allah's peace and blessings be upon him) said:

As long as one upon earth witnesses the existence of Allah in sincerity, the end of the world will not come.

As long as there is one single person who sees the macrocosm and himself as the microcosm, and witnesses the Creator of which he is the proof, then

... *kullun min 'indi Llah.* ...
... all is from Allah. ...

(Nisa', 4:78)

O Lord, sustain my being with certainty, keep me safe from the mischief of my evil ego. For all power, all ability, belong only to Allah Most High.

CHAPTER V

The Nature of Reality

Know that what exists is the Truth.

Allah is the absolute existence that contains all the Divine and beautiful attributes in their absolute perfection. He is the essence and the cause of all existence; yet He does not in any way resemble any of His creatures. "Allah" is only Allah's name; yet nothing else can in any way assume even His name, nor share it.

He is before the before; He did not become; He always was.

He is after the after, eternal; He always will be.

He is unique without partner, without resemblance. All is in need of Him. All has become by His order, "Be," and dies and disappears by His order.

He is the Creator, bearing no resemblance to the creation.

He is Self-Existent, without any needs.

Allah is perfection; the extent of His perfection is infinite. He is ever-living, all-knowing, all-hearing, all-seeing. All will is His; all power is His, all existence and action depend on Him. The word, all that is said and taught, is His.

All perfection in its totality is visible in His creation, but it is not Him, it is from Him.

What appears as inharmonious within the visible world is dis-

The Nature of Reality

cord between the appearances, not in the One who appears, for disharmony or harmony only occur between things in multiplicity. Multiplicity is in appearances, not in the One who appears.

Yet appearances are not other than the One who appears. What one sees depends on who is looking. A person sees other than what is because of the veils over his eyes. What he sees is the image, not the reality.

Only those who know reality see the Reality. They see the Reflected in the reflections, the Named in the names. The difference between the seen and He Who Is Seen is in the images, not in the Reality, Who is One.

Allah the One and Unique is manifested in all that is seen. Although these manifestations may appear unrelated, in reality they are the same. They may appear to have their own particularities, but in essence all is one. This is Allah's being, His truth.

If each and every thing in its reality claimed, "I am the Truth," it would not be a lie, because everything is from Him. Nor is there multiplicity in these many truths, because they are the same, the One Truth, the Source. Yet in their appearances, each thing has a name of its own. Therefore it is not right that each be called "Truth."

The names of the Creator are made distinct from and other than the names of the created. It is impermissible to attribute the name of the cause to the effect. When the weather is calm, an ocean is an ocean; when there is a storm it turns into waves. In reality it is still the ocean.

In essence there is neither multiplicity nor difference among things. Multiplicity is an illusion. There is neither change nor transformation: change is a stage in progression; it is unable to encompass the whole. That is what the blessed Prophet (may Allah's peace and blessings be upon him) meant when he said:

kana Llahu wa lam yakun ma'ahu shay'in, wa huwa 'alani ma 'alayhi kana.

Allah existed and nothing else existed with Him, and He is now as He was.

And Allah says:

kullu shay'in halikun illa wajhahu

Everything will perish but His essence.

(Qasas, 28:88)

Some of Allah's attributes are given to His creation. They are Divine secrets placed within the creation. When placed in temporal existences they become subject to influences. They are called the Beautiful Names of the Created. If they are divulged, the veils of Divine secrets will be torn, and these attributes will lose their connection with the One who placed them in His creation. The one who divulges the secret will be punished, and the greatest punishment is to become disconnected from the Creator, to fall out of His favor and protection.

When al-Hallaj (may Allah sanctify his secret) said, "I am the Truth"—which he was—he lost his connection with the Truth, because the Divine truth in him, when exposed, was influenced, changed, and misunderstood. For this he was punished by torture and execution in this world, and by isolation from the ones whom he loved in the Hereafter.

To call Truth something that has been identified by a name and limited by that name is sacrilege. Humanity, and even beast, plant, and rock—when they are not seen, when they do not exist in multiple forms—may be called "Truth." When they come into existence and become *a* man, *an* animal, or *a* plant, they are created things, within which the Truth is hidden. They cannot be called "the Truth."

* * *

The Nature of Reality

This world pulls people in two directions. It leads some to the Truth and some to what is other than the Truth. Therefore, this life in this world is both true and not true. It is lawful to be worldly, for one may seek the Truth in the world; on the other hand it may be unlawful to be worldly when it leads one to forget the Truth.

A shaikh was asked, "How do you deal with the world; how do you reconcile the worldly with the divine?"

He answered, "As novices we strive to ascend from the worldly to the Truth. As mature men, we descend from the Truth to the world, with the Truth."

Men are like trees in a forest to be cut for firewood. Some, who are dry, catch fire with a spark and do not go out. They turn into pure fire and are consumed. As it is said in a tradition of the Prophet (may Allah's peace and blessings be upon him),

idha tummal-faqru, fa-huwa Llah.

When poverty is complete, there is Allah.

This means Allah manifests Himself in the one whose heart has been purified when his being is totally consumed. These are they who have the potential of unity.

In the forest of humanity there are also some trees that are green, full of sap. They will not burn unless they lose their sap. Before they are to be used for firewood, they must be seasoned. Even then, they hardly burn, and most of the wood is left after the fire is out.

Some men are like this green wood. They will scorch, but they will stay wood. No matter how one attends to them, the effort is useless; they will not change.

In this forest there are other trees which, although green, have sap like resin. They catch fire easily. If you attend to them, they will keep burning. If not, they will go out. You cannot leave them alone. Someone must occupy themselves with them always. Then, in time, they also may be consumed.

Most ordinary men are like this. They are attached to this world, proud of themselves, creatures of habit; but if someone helps them to get rid of their many "I's" and "me's" and "mine's"—helps them to burn to ashes—they may also reach a state of unity. However, they cannot be left to their own ways.

* * *

Pure truth, the only existence, is Allah's essence, which is pure and exempt from anything; yet everything is in it and from it; and everything is in need of it. Nothing is apart from it. Although Allah is exempt from anything visible, yet He is within the seen as well as the unseen.

That vision is not an image seen by the eye of the head but a spiritual vision seen by the eye of the heart. It is the reality of what we call reality, which in itself is only an illusion. The True Reality of all reality is nothing other than He. He is the cause; things are His effect. The truth within the effect is He. The effect is created because Allah is manifested in it.

In His essence Allah is the self-existent causal necessity. The visible effect of this—the creation within the realm of possibility—receives its attributes from Him because what is created, which is only a possibility, can have no existence by itself.

Allah describes this with a metaphor in the Holy Qur'an:

marajal-bahrayni yaltaqiyan baynahuma barzakhun la yabghiyan

> He has made the two seas to flow freely, meeting together. Between them is a barrier which they do not transgress.
>
> (Rahman, 55:19-20)

The Nature of Reality

The *two seas* are the sea of the causal necessity and the sea of the effected possibility. The *two seas flowing freely, meeting together* are the state of unity when both exist in one being. (The *barrier* is Allah's essence, which *they do not transgress*). They neither undo nor change each other, although they are neither the same as nor resemble each other. The causal truth cannot be the effected possibility; nor can the possible effect be the Truth. Yet they are the same existence, the one Truth, for there is no other existence than the Truth. The difference and separation between Creator and created, cause and effect, is nominal, imaginary, and hypothetical.

* * *

The One and Absolute Being is Allah the Creator. He is the cause. The effect of the cause is the creation. The Causal Existence, who is absolute and total, fashions all and everything with His two Hands of Grace and Might.

Thus He is manifest in everything; yet He is other than everything. Even if He is visible in billions of things and billions of ways, He is one, and in reality there is nothing but Him. Everything is from Him; He is manifest in everything.

The seeing and the one who is seen and the one who sees are the same. Any separation or difference between them is imaginary. Yet when the Truth is manifest in the creation, what is seen is not the essence of the One who is manifested. The Reality assumes the shape of the predisposition and capacity of the thing within which it is seen.

* * *

Allah's will and His wish are the requirements of His essence. People generally understand the manifestations of Allah's will simply as His doing or undoing, His creating or annihilating things that may possibly happen or cease to exist. They think His will is a choice between opposites. This is a reflection of the will of the created, which they relate to the Divine will. This is a false premise.

* * *

Allah says in His Holy Book:

fa-idha sawwaytuhu wa nafakhtu fihi min ruhi....

So when I have made him complete and breathed into him of My spirit....

(Hijr, 15:29)

The meaning of *when I have made him complete* is that when the human being is given the form particular to itself—when all its organs and the parts of its body are ready to function in perfection, when the desired effect of the breathing *into him of [His] spirit* is complete— then the soul will enter the body. But for the soul to enter the body, Allah must will it and breathe it in.

This spirit of Divine origin appears in man as man, in beast as beast, and in plant as plant. And it appears differently even within each species, appearing in each person in a different manner in accordance with his different capacity and predisposition.

The spirit which leaves the body upon death is not that appearance which became visible with the form that carried it. The spirit neither disappears nor diminishes nor changes when the body is destroyed.

The body, prior to its end, is in continuous transformation, while the spirit never changes. It cannot be identified by anything other than the body it inhabits. There is no identification without appearance; therefore, it is essential for the spirit to have a form. Yet if the spirit becomes fully identified with a specific body, it cannot return to its origin.

The Nature of Reality

This is why those who have attained the Truth are not restricted to one personal identity. They appear as everybody. The Divine wisdom they have been given crystallizes in the gift of an image of fine matter, and they are raised to the levels of the highest paradise while yet on earth.

On the other hand, those who disassociate and separate themselves from the Divine harmony, who revolt against Divine order, who do not know themselves and take their false personalities to be themselves—their poor souls take the shape of whatever beast's nature dominates them and they become identified with the animals, whose souls are lost with the loss of their bodies.

This is the difference between man and beast. Otherwise, their cause and origin is the same.

* * *

Know that Allah does not make known the secret of His essence.

Allah says:

wa yuhadhdhirukumu Llahu nafsahu

Allah warns you against Himself.

(Al 'Imran, 3:28)

This means Allah forbids you to think of His essence. His Prophet (may Allah's peace and blessings be upon him) said:

tafakkaru fi ati Llahi wa la tafakkaru fidh-dhati Llah.

Think of Allah's attributes and His Beautiful Names but do not try to find out His essence.

Allah and His Messenger forbid us to reflect upon His essence because our intelligence—which is also created by Allah and is also a Divine attribute manifest in us—is not sufficient to recognize the Essence. All that is possible for human beings is to reflect upon the manifestation of His Names, actions, and attributes in and around us, and by the little that we can see, to try and imagine His infinite greatness.

For all these images and their becoming depend on Him. They exist by the Truth, and they are seen by the Truth. Their reality is indeed within the essence of Allah. They are a part of it. Their existence is due to Allah's essence—but it is impossible to know that essence.

* * *

To seek the Truth, to arrive at the Truth, is no more than to seek and know reality. Things that are visible, concrete—whether perceived by the senses or conceived by the mind—are all similes, a likening of one thing to another, while the absolute truth is absolved of comparison and free from being understood by the senses and by the mind. The Holy Qur'an says:

laysa ka-mithlihi shay'un wa huwas-sami' ul-basir.

Nothing is like unto Him and He is the Hearing, the Seeing.

(Shura, 42:110)

There are two approaches to knowing Allah. One is to liken Him to something that we know—in this verse, *He is the Hearing, the Seeing*. The other way is to absolve Him of all likeness, as in *Nothing is like Him*.

There is some knowledge in similes, and that is knowledge of His attributes. Whenever He is likened to anything, there is no direct knowledge. An image reflected in a mirror is outside the mirror. If Allah is manifest in His creation, we can understand that He is other than His creation. He is free of any resemblance to anything and is other than His creation; yet His creation is His reflection.

A shadow is outside of the thing that casts the shadow. The one who casts the shadow is not in need of it; yet the shadow is due to the one who casts it. The creation is like Allah's shadow. If there were no God there would be no existence, but Allah is Ever-Existent. He could exist without His creation. He is the Absolute Being. He is the Self-Existent whose existence is necessary for the existence of others.

Hadrat Mevlana Jalaluddin Rumi wrote in his *Divani-Kabir*:

Care not about the bowing and the prostration
   of the shadow,
For the shadow has no will or purpose.
Do not take it to be alive, although the Everliving
   One casts it.
I move as He moves. I stand still when He stops.
Neither do I have a thing, nor do I have it not.
How dare I speak, for a shadow cannot,
Until perchance He moves His lips and says "He."

The causal being first appeared as minute elements which formed boiling lava and mountains, then grew from them as plants, then appeared as animals, then finally as man.

I was a hidden secret. I loved to be known.
With the love of my Maker I burst into flames.
I am the sun, the moon, and all the stars
   spreading light, and the constellations
     by which to find your path.
My atoms became nature, my soul the *adhan*.
As I traveled whirling around my axis, I became

> the space and time and the place of return.
> I burst into all colors as plants and flowers. I went
> into the shape of beasts and kept silent
> about my secret.
> Now I rest within the palace of the image of man.
> I am called by my Lord a thousand and one
> names.
> I translate them into the language of all creation.
> My shape is that of my invisible soul, the shadow
> He casts on the whole universe.
> All that my Maker made is here in me. I am the
> before, the now, and all that ever will be.
> Beware, Hulusi, do not divulge the secret of your
> Lord's command when He said "Be," and
> all became!
> (From Hajji Hulusi Maqsud's *Divan*)

The sole owner of all these forms and shapes is the causal being, the Lord of the universe. If all disappeared, nothing would be left except Him.

When man eats an apple or an animal, that apple and beast become a part of man. They change from the state of animal or vegetable into the state of man. What a human being takes from without, by his own choice changes his being in turn.

In the same manner, the essential being evolves from one state to another, one level to another. Because of this transformation, Hadrat 'Ali (may Allah be pleased with him) said:

> I am the Pen and the Heavenly Tablet. I am the
> Throne and the Footstool of my Lord.

The greatest of all shaikhs, Muhyiddin Ibn 'Arabi (may Allah sanctify his secret) wrote in his book *The Bezels of Wisdom*:

If you say your Lord is unlike anything, you limit Him.

If you liken Him to His creation, you restrict Him.

If you can see Him both unlike and like His creation, you will see the truth.

And in knowing Him you will be a guide and a master.

To know and remember your Lord is both to see His manifestations and to know that you cannot see Him but that He sees you. You must see His attributes with your mind and senses, and you must use your heart and your feeling to have faith in the One, invisible and unimaginable, who is unlike anything else. Then you may be lifted to the state of inspiration which is the level of the truth of Muhammad.

CHAPTER VI

The Reality of Muhammad

The affirmation of the truth of Muhammad is in Chapter Bani Isra'il (17:34) where Allah says:

wa la taqrabu mal al-yatimi illa billati hiya ahsanu hata yablugha ashudah. . . .

And draw not nigh to the orphan's property except in a goodly way, until he attains maturity. . . .

The word *orphan* refers to the Prophet (May Allah's peace and blessings be upon him) and the *property* of the orphan is the truth contained in him. The *attaining of maturity* is the level of perfect man as exemplified in the Prophet Muhammad (May Allah's peace and blessings be upon him). Coming close to Truth can be done only in *a goodly way* and by following in the footsteps of the Prophet (May Allah's peace and blessings be upon him).

When the prophet Moses (upon him be peace) aspired to see the Truth, and begged Allah:

rabbi arini anzur ilayka. . . .

My Lord, show me Yourself so that I may look at You. . . .

(A'raf, 7:143)

Allah said:

lan tarani, wa-lakin inzur ilal-jabali, fa-inni istaqarra makanahu fa-sayfa tarani.

You cannot see Me. But look at the mountain, I will show Myself to it. If it remains firm in its place, then you will see Me.

(A'raf, 7:143)

Allah is giving a warning to the prophet Moses (upon him be peace). Moses spoke to Him and heard Him and thus knew the Truth in words, but he wished to see the Truth and be a witness. However, one's material being is as coarse as a mountain and cannot stand the weight of the Truth. If the Truth is manifested upon it, it will crumble.

Allah says:

fa-lamma tajalla rabbuhu lil-jabali, ja'lahu dakkan.

So when his Lord manifested His glory to the mountain, He made it crumble.

He was showing Moses (upon him be peace) that if you hold onto material being—if the mountain is to stand—you will only be able to see Him in relation to your own identity, not in Himself.

* * *

The Reality of Muhammad is the reflection of Allah's Truth. As the Prophet Muhammad (May Allah's peace and blessings be upon him) said:

man ra'ani fa-qad ra'al-haqq.
Whoever sees me certainly has seen the Truth.

You cannot come to Truth, you with yourself. You have to annihilate yourself, as the mountain of matter was annihilated.

You and the whole universe of matter, like the pile of rock a mountain is, are a three-dimensional distorted image of Truth. The two-dimensional base of the flattened mountain is closer to Truth, as close as a shadow to that which casts the shadow. Yet it has no being; it is not real. The only being is the Reality of Muhammad, and the real Reality is the Truth.

* * *

When the mountain crumbled, when the material being of Moses was lost—

wa harra Musa sa'iqa

. . . and Moses fell down in a swoon. . . .

—his awareness of his existence, his very name, and all and everything that he took as Moses, disappeared.

fa-lamma afaqa

When he recovered. . . .

He came back in another state, in the state of a mirror that reflects *an-nur al-Muhammadi*, the light of Truth, seeing himself

The Reality of Muhammad

with the eye of his soul rather than the eye of the head. He said:

subhanaka tubtu ilayka wa ana awwal ul-mu'minin

Glory be to You! I turn to you in repentance and I am the first of the believers.

(A'raf, 7:143)

He meant: "I see You not through myself but through You, and I came to this state by repenting of wanting to see You by myself. I am the first to realize that only You can see Yourself by Yourself."

* * *

Allah first created the causal existence in the form of a great light. It is called the Light of Muhammad, *muhammad* meaning "the most praised one"; his other name is *hamid*, the only one who is given the ability to praise and give thanks to Allah. That first existence from which all existence came to be is the manifestation of Allah.

When Muhammad (May Allah's peace and blessings be upon him) came upon this world in the most perfect form of man, he was brought to his Lord during his lifetime in an ascension called *mi'raj*, when he saw his Lord through his Lord. The mystery of his ascension is explained in Allah's words:

wa idh qulna laka inna rabbaka ahata bin-nas. . . .

When We said to you, "Surely thy Lord encompasses men. . . ."

(Bani Isra'il, 17:60)

For man does not have an existence. He is covered by his Lord.

Inspirations

What people take for themselves are nothing other than the shadows of Allah's attributes. A shadow is an illusion; it does not exist.

The immaterial soul of man is together with Allah. That is what hears and sees Allah through Allah. Man can see the spirit with the spiritual eye. The physical eye sees only the shadow, the darkness, the veil that hides the truth.

wa la surata li-Adami fa-la wujuda illa wa huwa 'ayn al-haqq

There is no form to man, no reality. The only reality is that of Allah.
 (Ibn 'Arabi, *Bezels of Wisdom*)

And the Reality of Muhammad is its reflection, which is the Truth.

* * *

Absolute being is the essence of Allah Most High. In the degrees of knowledge of Allah, there are always two considerations of the one and unique existence. At each stage of the understanding of Allah one must consider both the influence of the causal existence—His actions, His doings—and the effect of these influences and actions.

When He is known as the Cause, we call Him "God," "Allah." When we know Him by His effects we call Him "the universe, the existences, the creation, the things that come to be visible, conceivable, not Him but from Him."

When we establish that these reflections of His attributes within the perceivable universe exist by Him and come from Him but are variable and temporal, the necessity of the two considerations in the understanding of the one becomes clear.

If one sees the cause and effect separately, one's self being the

The Reality of Muhammad

microcosm of the creation, one understands and describes Him in terms of appearances, the visible God, but there are great dangers in this.

If one associates the effect with the cause as a reference, a similitude, enabling one to compare and consider the effect together with the cause, the danger of confusion is less.

If one is able to see the cause and effect as one, one has seen the true identity of Allah. One's spirit and body become one: one sees the Truth; one speaks the Truth; one becomes the Truth.

Thus, when you remember Him, dissociate Him from His reflection upon the universe that you know with your senses. If you can, associate the Cause, His essence, with the reflection of His beautiful attributes in your heart.

* * *

The spiritual is not separate from the concrete. Yet spirituality should not be attributed to the concrete, nor concreteness to the spiritual. Hadrat 'Ali (may Allah be pleased with him) has said:

> * *al-tafriqatu bila jam'in ishrak.* (Those who see existence as other than and separate from Allah are in a state of *shirk*, attributing partners to Allah, the unforgivable sin.)
>
> * *wal-jam'un bila tafriqatin zandaqah.* (Those who think that existence is the same as Allah have invented their own religion.) They think that the visible material world is Allah and deny the possibility of any other being. They have devised for themselves very convincing theories and proofs dependent on what is visible and tangible as to the absolute truth of their belief.
>
> * *wal-jam'u wal-tafriqu tawhid.* (Those who are able to both associate and dissociate, who can view the world and Allah as separate and at the same time as

one, have achieved unity.)
They have become aware of their souls. Allah describes them:

la-qad khalaqnal-insanu fi-ahsani taqwim.

We have created (the soul of) man in the most beautiful, best, most perfect form.

(Tin, 95:4)

Such people have the secret of all existence within themselves. They have found themselves to be one with all being, thus reaching the state of losing themselves in Allah, achieving unity.

Allah has manifested His reality in His creation. Creation is the evolution of spirit into body. Nothing is created from nothing. There is a cause and an effect, an essence and an appearance of the essence. Hajji Bayram Wali (may Allah sanctify his secret) wrote in one of his poems:

> My Lord built a city between the two worlds.
> When I looked I saw myself in it.
> Suddenly I found myself in it, as it was being built,
> And I was put in the mortar between its bricks.

* * *

If there were no causal existence or the apparent existences that are its effects, if these had not been relative to us and to our understanding, then nothing would have existed. Existence is the total of the cause and the effect and of the one who perceives it.

When men worship, they worship with their material being. In human beings the effect of the cause recognizes the cause. The worshipper and the worshipped are Him; His appearance worships His essence. Yet the worshipper is temporal and has limits; the worshipped is eternal and absolute.

The Reality of Muhammad

It is sacrilegious for a temporal being to worship something temporal, except on occasions when Allah chooses one of His temporal attributes to be considered as a sign of His existence.

One such case is the turning toward the Ka'bah in the city of Mecca, which is considered the house of God.

Another is the case of Adam (upon him be peace). Allah ordered the angels to prostrate in front of Adam because He had taught him all His names, thus giving him the knowledge of all creation.

In such cases the temporal existence becomes a pointer to Him, and the prostration to the created object becomes the worship of the One who created it.

Let not such signs become veils between you and the Truth. He is visible in everything that He has created, and He has set no veils between Him and His creation. It is your blindness, your ignorance, and your imagination that become a barrier between you and Him.

Hadrat Shibli (may Allah sanctify his secret) said, "I imagined the beauty of Layla behind her bridal veils, but when I saw Layla, her beauty had no veils, and her beauty was more wonderful than I had imagined, and I understood that the veils were my eyelids and the beauty behind the closed eyes, in my imagination, was insufficient."

* * *

The eight essential attributes of the perfection of Allah are:

* the Everliving One,
* the All-knowing One,
* the All-hearing One,
* the All-seeing One,
* the One Upon Whose Will All Is Dependent,
* the Absolute Power,
* the One Upon Whom All Actions and Existence Depend,

* the Word That Contains All That Is Said.

These attributes are manifest in you, His most perfect creation—but you think that they are *your* qualities and believe that you have characteristics in common with your Lord!

You take yourself for another god, thinking that there is a "you" and a "Him," both with the same attributes, while your Lord has entrusted you with His Names as a sign so that you can know Him— and as a proof that only He exists.

One of the attributes of Allah is the Creator. It is particular to Him and is manifest in all and everything. No human being, nothing in the whole creation, can attribute this name to himself. You can say that you have power, will, knowledge, and the ability to see, hear, and speak words, but you cannot say, "I am the creator." The ones who consider themselves "creative" are the fortunate ones whom Allah has rendered able to act in accordance with His will. So the attribute of the Creator is an attribute that dissociates the Creator from all of the created.

The attribute of the Word— containing all that is said—is reflected only in humanity, out of the whole of creation. None other than man can put his thoughts, his feelings, into words. Here is an attribute that associates the Creator with the human being, while separating Him from the rest of creation.

When man attempts to know Allah through what is made manifest in him from Him, he is bound to see that none of these Divine attributes—or actions which come through him, or things done by his hands—are his. Everything belongs to Allah, including himself. Then he will realize that his very existence is through the existence of Allah. In Allah he will come to love Allah.

Hadrat Ibn Farid (may Allah sanctify his secret) wrote:

> O man, until you lose yourself in Him,
> You will not come to love Him,
> And until He shows Himself in you,
> You will not come to lose yourself in Him.

When you admit that you are created, the Creator is manifest in you. You should see that you are not "yourself" but His manifestation—for truly, the name and the named are one and the same. You must also never forget that while you are from Him, you are not Him.

As you come closer to Allah, you will come to know Truth as it is manifested in you, and you will be perfected. Perfection is the manifestation of Allah's most beautiful name, the Beneficent, the One who wills mercy and good for all creation at all times without any distinction between the righteous and the sinner, the loved and the hated. He pours infinite bounties upon all creation. As it is described in the Qur'an:

wa rahmati wasi'at kulla shay'in

My mercy covers everything.

(A'raf, 7:156)

When His beloved Prophet Muhammad (May Allah's peace and blessings be upon him) said, "*inni la-ajidu ya'tina rih ur-Rahman min qabl il-Yaman* (I smell the perfume of the Beneficent One from the direction of Yemen), he meant the perfect man of the time, Uways al-Qarani, whose love for him and for Allah dominated everything else in him. Allah Most High says:

thumm astawa 'alal-'arsh, ar-Rahmanu. . . .

The All-Merciful, Beneficent One is established upon the Throne (is in power over all the heavens).

(Furqan, 25:59)

The perfect man, in whom the All-Merciful is manifest, rules over all the levels of Creation. There are three Thrones, three major

levels of Creation:
> * the "heaven of grace" where the Truth becomes manifest;
> * the "heaven of glory" which is the level of substitution where the perfect man, in whom all Allah's attributes are manifest, rules in His name; and
> * the "heaven of power" which encompasses all other heavens.

The visible existence which we call the universe is not separated from or other than the Divine Being. He is the owner of the universe because the universe is dependent upon Him. In the physical existence of human beings, which is temporal and limited, the eternal limitless soul resides in and owns the body, which is then dependent upon it. When this is realized, no conflict or opposition from your ego will take hold upon you. Your soul will be the master of your ego, and you will not be the slave of your ego.

* * *

The necessity for unity in the multiplicity of the visible world, as in the multiplicity within oneself, is the will of the Lord. It is a sign of His existence. One may realize and taste the unity of all things, and the oneness of the Creator and the created, with an effort similar to the effort of achieving unity within oneself—yet much greater than that.

When a man is unified and his many "I's" have become one "I," when he sees that his many aspects are dependent on that one "I," he runs the danger of imagining that he has "achieved" the truth, having become "the same as" the Truth.

A human being reaches the state of unity through remembrance, by consciousness of himself and of his state. However, it is not an end in itself. Such a state is like the state of Majnun, the lover of an imagined Layla, when they showed him the real Layla.

"Here is Layla, your beloved!" they told him. He said, "No, that is not Layla. I am Layla!" and ran away from her into the mountains to be alone.

Such a state is indeed a state of purity, a state of seclusion, a state in which the one who remembers and the one who is remembered and the remembrance become one, the lover and the beloved and love become one. But it is still not the final goal of the unification of the Creator and the created. It is a sign of it, a taste of it. That is why it is said that it cannot be described. The one who has not tasted it can never know it.

* * *

There are three levels of knowledge. First there is knowledge obtained through intermediaries—a fact reported by others. Then there is knowledge through experience—a fact seen, touched, tasted. And then there is true knowledge, in which one becomes that which is experienced.

The unification of the self is the state of seeing the sign of Divine unity. It is "I, seeing Him." There is duality in it.

In duality there is no certainty as to which is the One. When I know that I am myself, all that I can say about Him is that "perhaps" He is Himself.

To truly know Him you must realize the "He" and lose the "I."

These states cannot be achieved alone. There have to be proofs of reality being reality. That is why one needs a guide, a guide who has been there and can lead you there. Whoever finds the true guide has found the truth.

There are signs, proofs of the true guide. The clearest sign is his truthfulness, his total sincerity.

Someone may worship day and night, may know all your past and the secrets of your future, may know the outer and the inner secrets of all and everything, perform miracles, walk on air. If he is not sincere, you must keep away from him.

Such miracles can be induced; sorcerers can perform them. The true miracle is the miracle of the knowledge of Allah, and belongs to the ones who have been with Him.

They are the perfect teachers. When you see them, you will know them for they revive dead hearts. When the heart is alive, it can only beat for the love of the One who created it. Its sign is a sign of peace: the concerns and the troubles of the world leave your heart or are seriously reduced, so that you are in awe, in ecstasy, in love in His presence.

These real teachers are united within themselves, united with all and everything, and united with the Truth. Therefore they know unity well.

* * *

The knowledge of unity is of three kinds.

The first is a knowledge obtained through study, a rational understanding of the unity within the multiplicity learned through books, from teachers, secondhand, from the experience of others. Most theologians have obtained their knowledge by these means. When the Prophet (May Allah's peace and blessings be upon him) said:

> *al-'ulama'u wuratha' ul-anbiya', wa kullu 'ulama'i ummati kan-nabiyya bani Isra'il*
>
> Men of knowledge are the inheritors of the knowledge of the prophets. The men of knowledge of my people are like the prophets of the Israelites [who received their knowledge from God's words].

he was explaining the level of the knowledge of unity.

The knowledge of unity obtained through conscience is a state reached through the warnings and the orders of one's conscience, an inner discriminating state which has opted for unity over multiplicity. It is attained though inspiration, sometimes through dreams. This knowledge can sometimes be attained even by nonbelievers who are then brought to faith through it. This is a knowledge through seeing, by direct experience. It is rare and difficult. It becomes much easier if one follows a perfect guide and accepts him, his orders and warnings, as one's own conscience. Connecting one's heart to him, one will be able to receive the inner consciousness and awareness of unity firsthand through his help.

The third kind of knowledge of unity is through wish. This is an absolute faith that unity is a necessity, a total need—a yearning, enveloping one's whole being, excluding all other needs. It is this state which brings the exclusion and the disappearance of everything else, brings one to be one with the One. It is a knowledge neither through understanding nor experiencing but through being. And it is unique. Therefore it cannot be explained to the ones who have not tasted it.

This is the highest form of knowledge and the true goal.

CHAPTER VII

The Mystics

On the mystic path there are seven steps.
The first is orthodoxy, the following of Divine law.
The second is understanding and acting and living in accordance with Divine law.
The third is a state of sincerity and the finding of truth.
The fourth is the attainment of Divine knowledge.
The fifth is the realization of the essence in which everything is centered, a state of power where all becomes dependent upon a common pole, a state of unification.
The sixth is a state of spiritual intimacy of the created with the Creator.
The seventh is becoming a true servant of Allah. It is the goal, the highest state to which a created being can aspire.
On that last level the path of mysticism reaches its summit. It is complete. A descent to the creation with the intention of service begins.
However, when the mystic servant descends among the common people to serve them, he comes with knowledge that other eyes have not seen, or other ears heard, knowledge that cannot be imagined. He can only divulge that which people can understand: the rest he has to keep a secret. He has to appear like other people; yet he is different from them. It is a state of necessary hypocrisy. For if the mystic servant were to divulge his secrets to others whom he intends to serve, his words would be misconstrued. They would

not correspond to what others know or are able to understand, and other people would be incapable of putting those words into action. The mystic would risk accusations, persecution, even death at the hands of the ones whom he came to serve.

Hadrat 'Ali (may Allah be pleased with him) addressed his Lord, saying, "O Lord, if I were to spread the treasures of Your knowledge among people they would accuse me of being an idol-worshipper. The very believers would think it lawful to kill me and would approve the worst treatment of me."

Hadrat Abu Hanifah said, "I received two knowledges from the Messenger of Allah. I acted upon and lived according to one knowledge, taught it and spread it among people. If I had even mentioned the other, they would have cut my throat."

That is why a mystic must appear other than he is.

* * *

A great shaikh, Sari al-Saqati, said:

A mystic has one of three appearances. First, he may appear as a man of wisdom from whom the light of Divine knowledge is reflected. This light is so awesome that he fears nothing, for he who fears Allah is feared by all. Everyone loves him, for the one who loves Allah is loved by everyone and everything.

Second, he may appear as a hidden secluded mystic who does not divulge his inner knowledge, for he may know things that are hidden even in the Divine books and are beyond that which is evident and understood by all.

Finally the mystic may appear as an orthodox religious teacher following the religious canons, leading people to do what Allah orders in His Holy Books and preventing them from things that Allah forbids.

He keeps Allah's secret knowledge to himself.

Those who divulge the least of Allah's secrets to the ones who are unworthy to receive them meet harsh punishment, not only at the hands of the people, but from their Lord, risking even their faith.

* * *

What are miracles? The true miracles are phenomena, hitherto unknown, produced by knowledge—such as scientific discoveries. If such a miracle is to be attributed to someone, it must depend upon the findings and conscious efforts and knowledge of that person.

The "supernatural" phenomena displayed by someone who flies in the air or walks on water are gifts given to particular chosen servants of Allah. These demonstrations show people who are faithless and rendered blind by the illusions of this world (which they take to be reality) that things that they think of as supernatural exist.

Once a pious man was out strolling with his student when the student said, "Master, I hear that certain wise men pass from one place to another in a miraculous way, regardless of distance."

The master answered, "So do we! Don't you see that we are walking?"

The miracles that appear through pious guides to strengthen the faith of others are isolated and not continuous. They appear when the need appears and stop when their purpose is achieved or failed. They also stop if the pious person loses his piety or his intention of saving others.

The miracles of the mystic are contained in the knowledge within him and are continuous. He has obtained them through his own conscious experience. They are a part of him, one with him. When and if he demonstrates these miracles, there is no dissociation between the miracle and the producer of the miracle. Therefore they are never merely for show. The only time they may appear to be for show is when they do not seem to correspond to their producer—in the eye of a beholder who is cross-eyed and sees the one as two!

For instance, if you tell people who are partially blind, who see only a fraction and take it for all of reality, that this world is created, they may agree with you—except that what you mean and what they understand are two different things. They will agree with you even more if you say that visible existence is the reality, the absolute truth. In both cases you will be right, and although they agree with you, they will be wrong.

Their view is limited: they see only part of truth, and it is this limitation that becomes the cause of their disbelief. Even if they accept a God, they limit him with this world, while Allah is limitless and timeless: He existed before there was any existence and will exist after there is none. It is not that these people take the sun, the moon, and the stars as gods. It is that they take Him to be merely the god of the sun, the moon, and the stars. Their sight is limited; therefore, their God is limited. Each of their concepts of reality is different, therefore each of their Gods is different.

In *al-Futuhat al-Makkiyah*, Hadrat Muhyiddin ibn al-'Arabi said:

Everyone believes in another thing as the Lord. My belief contains all their beliefs and more.

* * *

The ultimate knowledge is the realization of unity, but the three steps necessary to achieve this are also applicable to the achievement of all knowledge. These steps are knowledge through indirect means, knowledge through personal experience, and knowledge through being one with knowledge.

For instance, if you wish to know about generosity and courage, your intention must be to become generous and courageous.

If you hear from others what generosity is and about the generosity of others, it is not of much use if you do not intend to apply this knowledge to yourself but only to tell others what you have heard. Allah likens people who acquire knowledge and are unable to act upon it to donkeys carrying heavy books.

It is not always easy to believe totally in what one hears from others. It is easier to believe in things that one observes oneself. Knowledge depending on one's own experience—the witnessing of acts of generosity or courage—is more direct. Even so, the experience one can have of the generosity and courage of others is limited. The reality of generosity and courage is much larger.

One may understand oneself to be a part of reality and, as such, not to differ from reality, just as a drop of water from the ocean is neither the ocean nor other than the ocean. In that state one experiences generosity and courage in themselves, in oneself.

Each of these steps is taken by oneself, and they are called real knowledge. Although they are not the Knowledge, they are not other than it. They are not the Truth, but they are from the Truth.

The realization of unity is attained in a similar manner.

If you believe that there is nothing other than the God who created you and everything else, including all actions and states, and if you learned this from wise teachers, prophets, or Divine books—you know the unity of Allah by hearsay.

If you become able to see unity in the multiplicity around yourself and if you are able to bring the many "I's" in yourself into a single "I," then you will know unity through direct experience.

If you come to realize that nothing—not even yourself—exists at all save through the existence of the One, then you will have truly realized the unity of Allah.

* * *

The mystic spends time and effort in remembrance, trying to be conscious. It is a part of his discipline. The discipline of remembrance includes the act of remembrance, the one who remembers, and that which is remembered.

The first step for a novice is to understand and accept that the remembrance, the one who remembers, and the one who is remembered are all one. He knows this and accepts it because he was informed of it by his teacher.

When the student becomes conscious of himself in these exercises, then the rememberer, the remembrance, and the remembered become one as a personal experience.

These first two steps are dependent on one's physical, material self—upon one's ability to reason, to feel.

The third and final step, although arrived at through the previous steps, is a state of inspiration and comes both from within and from without. It takes place when the one who remembers disappears in the one remembered.

The mystic first pronounces the name of the Remembered. This is an external act in which the word of remembrance becomes the sound, the image of the Remembered One.

The next state, the true remembrance, is an inner state in which the heart, the essence, takes the invisible form of the Remembered One. The essence is one with the Reality; it is the Reality.

The beautiful names of Allah, chanted, are like a wind that creates waves on the surface of an ocean. At first one identifies the sea with these waves. Then one sees the waves as the *surface* of the deep ocean. The waves sink into the sea; the wind stops; the surface is calm. The ocean is one body. So the heart of the rememberer becomes calm and unified, and the chanting of the word is not heard, for it sinks into the depths of one's soul and covers not only one's whole being but all and everything.

Two objects of remembrance cannot fit into the heart at the same time, for the heart immediately *becomes* that which it remembers. A remembered thing completely fills it, so whatever penetrates it will be the only thing it *can* remember.

CHAPTER VIII

Manifestation of the Inner Self

Sometimes you will feel that you have become beautiful, and that feeling is so intense that you appear beautiful, though the beauty is too delicate, too refined to be seen and appreciated by the eye. You will be aware that, although it is an inner beauty, it becomes manifest in your physical being.

Although the soul and the body have nothing in common, there is no doubt that the soul manifests itself though the body. This happens when your refined invisible state becomes dense, appearing on the surface of your physical self. It is like humidity which is invisible; as it becomes dense it becomes visible as clouds. The invisible wetness in things is not a different substance from the clouds. They are the same. When the refined becomes coarser, it accumulates; it becomes visible and beautiful. When the invisible becomes visible, nothing is added to it.

Thus the beauty that is seen in your physical self is nothing other than the manifestation of your inner beauty. It is but the materialization through density of the refined matter that the soul is.

Yet at the same time, the cloud is not identical with the invisible humidity in all things; the wave upon the ocean is not the ocean; your body is not your soul. It is like the shadow of your soul, its apparition.

As the Messenger of Allah said,

arwahukum ashbahukum, ashbahukum arwahukum

Your soul is your appearance and your appearance is your soul.

Sometimes, when you are in a meditative state, you may receive a clear inner observation that captures your whole being. Even if you try to rid yourself of it, you cannot. It is like a waking dream. Or this may happen to you in dreams during your sleep. The next day, or soon enough, that feeling or dream appears to you in real life.

The Messenger of Allah said,

lam yabka min an-nubuwwati illal-mubashshirat

Nothing will remain of prophethood except true dreams.

Such visions of the unseen are as real as inspirations from the Lord. Indeed in all prophets the beginning of revelation came with dreams.

Pure dreams, true dreams, are a light from the Divine light of Allah. This light enables those who experience it to see Reality. Indeed it carries a part of the quality of prophethood. Dreams come from realms and times unseen by the eye, and therefore the images in them do not correspond to what we know. Yet these images contain hidden realities important to understand, especially for people seeking the truth.

One night as we were praying I was enveloped by a light that blinded me. I was bound by that light. I saw in it things that could not be seen by the eye. I received divine secrets. I felt intense pain and great pleasure at the same time, and these words poured from my lips:

ya nafsi sabbihi abadan
ya nafsi muti hamadan
wa la tahinni ahadan
illa jalilan samadan

O self, remember Allah without end.
O self, the death of this flesh is nothing more than
 the fading of worn clothes.
But I am contained in nothing other than the
 Glorious, the Eternal One.

I was in a gathering made up mostly of theologians. They were awed by my state. In fact, they were worried and afraid of the signs of pain I showed.

Among them was Mawlana Sayfuddin, one of the professors of the Barquqiyyah madrasah in Egypt. When I came to myself, I found myself looking at him. I did not see him as he appears ordinarily. I saw him in the shape of a spiritual teacher, more like myself than him, and I knew that I was looking into his reality. I saw our connection; I saw the oneness of the two of us.

CHAPTER IX

The Human Being

Allah says in His Holy Qur'an that

> *wal 'allama Adam al-asma'a kullaha thumma aradahum 'alal-mala'ikati fa-qala anbi'uni bi-asma'i ha'ula'i in kuntum sadiqin.*
> *qalu subhanaka la 'ilma lana illa ma 'allamtana innaka antal-'alimal-halim.*
> *qala ya Adamu anbi'hum bi-asma'ihim. . . .*

> He taught all the names to Adam; then He presented them to the angels. He said, "Tell me the names of these, if you are right." They said, "Glory be to thee; we have no knowledge but that which you have taught us. . . ."
> (Allah) said, "O Adam, inform them of their names."

(Baqarah, 2:31-33)

The names that Allah taught man are His own attributes, His Divine characteristics, which He places in man, and in accordance with which He wishes man to live.

His teaching the names to man also means that He has put the whole of creation, the entire universe, in the control of man. For a thing exists when it has a name, and the one who knows the name knows the nature of that thing and has control over it. Allah says in a Divine precept addressing man:

I have created everything for you and you for Myself.

Man, in whom Allah has placed His names, has the potential of knowing Allah through His attributes, of living in accordance with Divine morality and having the knowledge and control of the whole creation. When all this is realized in a person, he is a perfect human being.

The knowledge of the angels is inferior to the knowledge of a perfect man. They are only a means of communication through the materialization of Allah's invisible, infinite power. Through them the inner nature of matter, which is energy, becomes perceivable as the elements: earth, water, fire, and ether. They are the source through which the Divine energy becomes continuously apparent. Allah says:

tusabbihu lahus-samawatis-sab'u wal-ardu wa man fihinna.

The seven heavens and the earth and those in them declare His glory.

(Bani Isra'il, 17:44)

wa-in in shay's ill yusabbihu bi-hamdihi wa-lakin la tafkahuna tasbihahum. . . .

And there is not a single thing but glorifies Him with His praise, but you do not understand. . . .

(Bani Isra'il, 17:44)

Angels are the process of creation, the appearance of Allah's invisible energy in the forms, shapes, colors, perfumes, and sounds. Hadrat 'Ali (may Allah be pleased with him) said, "If you split the smallest particle of matter until the last divisible portion you

The Human Being

will find the sun in the center of it."

Angels are the glorification of their Divine cause. They are continuous in their appearance and existence, and that is the continual worship and praise attributed to them in the Qur'an. The constant glorification of the Creator by the created is the state of the angels.

The imperfect man, the heedless one who does not know himself or the Divine Names he contains, does not understand the language of the Divine spelled out in His creation. Neither does he understand the words of wisdom of the ones who see and know.

It is his attachment to the illusions of this world and of his imagination which renders him blind to reality. His imagination, which he takes to be reality, replaces reality. All that he "knows" has never happened. He is not in harmony with the Divine harmony. And as he rejects the truth, he is rejected by the truth.

If one were able to lift the heavy curtains of imagination, illusion, falsification, and heedlessness, the sign of this enlightenment would be the understanding and acceptance of the Divine messages and the words of the wise. One understands only that with which one agrees.

The beginning, in the process of consciousness, is to consider one's sins and one's errors as large and the good and the truth in one's actions as small. Thus one must make an effort to increase one's good deeds and a greater effort to reduce one's errors, which are produced by heedlessness and wrongs out of harmony with the Divine truth.

If one read the Holy Qur'an carefully, one would find that of the thirty sections, only one is about this world. The other twenty-nine are about the Hereafter. That should be the relative proportion of the efforts spent for this world (for one's material well-being) and for the Hereafter (for one's spiritual well-being).

Adam (upon him be peace) came out of Paradise into this world. Paradise is within the angelic realm. It is the glorious realm where the angels, the pure souls, and all the beautiful concepts reside.

Because all that Paradise contains is made out of pure light, of refined matter, it is invisible to the material eye. For the same reason, it is above material existence. Nothing from that realm can descend by itself, any more than a rock from this realm can ascend by itself.

Adam's (upon him be peace) expulsion from Paradise and descent to the earth happened when Divine energy threw him downward, just as an earthly rock must be thrown for it to go upwards. He was caught by the pull of matter. He lost his refined being and was condensed into the coarse matter that is our flesh.

If man does not dissociate his sight from his physical being—that is to say, if he tries to see Allah with his senses—he cannot see Him.

It is the perfect human being who separates his essence from the world and the worldly by decreasing his attachment to his flesh and the desires of his flesh, which are worldbound. Then he is attracted by the love of Allah.

As he sheds the weight of his physical being, his heart is lightened and purified and his essence ascends, pulled by the attraction of his beloved. And when Allah pulls him to Himself, all resistance is eliminated in him. This is the state of submission which is true Islam.

> ... *wa sara bi-ahlihi anasa min janibit-turi nara. qala li-ahlih-imkuthu inni anastu naran la'alli atikum minha bi-khayrin aw jadhwatin min an-nar la'allakum tastalun.*
>
> *fa-lama atayha nudiya min shatiril-wadi al-aymani al-mubarakati min ash-shajarati an ya Musa inni ana Llahu rabb ul-'alamin.*

[When Moses (upon him be peace)] was traveling with his family, he saw a fire on the side of the mountain. He said to his family, "Wait, I see a fire, maybe I will bring

The Human Being

from it a brand of fire so you may warm yourselves."

And when he came to it, he was called from the right side of the valley in the blessed spot of the bush, "O Moses, surely I am God, the Lord of the Worlds."

(Qasas, 28:29-30)

Moses (upon him be peace) was looking for fire but he found his Lord when the flaming bush said, "I am God."

The created universe is in the image of the Divine truth. It is not an image visible to the eye; it is a spiritual image, which addresses the spirit.

From whatever source, whatever created shape—if He cries, "I am God," it is true. He is the one who says it, and His declaration is His own. For the perfect human being who hears this declaration there is a sign, a sense of the relation between the Creator and the created, between spirit and form.

Although the word comes from the burning bush, the word is His and the bush is His. It is like a word pronounced by someone's lips—the word belongs neither to the lips nor to the tongue but to the essence of the person. If the tongue says, "I am a man," it is not the tongue who is a man.

As the words "I am God" came from a burning bush, they could also come from the tongue of a human being. Mansur al-Hallaj said, "I am the Truth." Indeed; every atom is the truth. The flaming bush did not have a self. When Hallaj said, "I am the Truth," there was no Hallaj.

Hadrat Maulana Jelaluddin Rumi explained this by saying, "When the iron is melted into a red fire, it is true to say that it is fire. But when it is cool and turns into solid iron, it is fire no longer."

When the creation, having lost its identity under the Divine power and manifestation, pronounces the words, "I am the Truth," it has no responsibility. Yet when it turns back to its identity, it must repent with its coarse being. And the one who hears such a declaration must not attribute divinity to either the burning bush or to the lips of the one who says, "I am the Truth."

The Prophet (may Allah's peace be upon him) said:

kana Llahu wa lam yakun ma'ahu shay'un.

Allah existed, and nothing existed with Him.

In the concept of the oneness of Allah, Allah is manifest in all of His creation. All existence is one. Part of it is outer, visible, and temporal. Part of it is inner, and some of it is eternal. However, in its existence it is all one, and in its becoming it is all eternal.

There is a level of understanding above the level of oneness. It is the level of uniqueness, as understood by that perfect man, the Prophet of Allah (may Allah's peace be upon him), when he said, "Allah existed and nothing existed with Him."

From the lips of the Prophet Muhammad (may Allah's peace be upon him) came Allah's injunction,

Mutu qabla an tamutu.

Die before you die.

Leave this world with your own will before you are faced with the necessity of leaving it at the end of your life, for whoever leaves the desires of his flesh and the tastes and the lust of this world will gain the eternal life as a reward for sacrificing the temporal.

There are three steps to achieving eternal life by dying to the world.

The first step is to protect oneself against the love, the ambition, the lust, the pleasures of this world, whose attractions pull us down to it and whose illusions distract us from Truth.

The second step is to try to live in strict accordance with the Divine precepts—not in a forced way but in seeking and assuming the Divine attributes, the beautiful names of Allah, and in making them one's character in sincerity. The most ordinary sort of example of this is that, when such a human being is dead and buried, beautiful memories of him live on.

The third and final step is to efface oneself, all that one has done and all that one was—including the Divine attributes with which one has characterized oneself, such as the Living One, the Hearing One, the Seeing One, the Knowing One, the Speaking One, the One with Power, the One with Will, the One who can create—all and everything, and to realize that there is no existence except Allah. There is no you, but only He. You are lost in Him, and you exist with Him. This is truly dying before dying.

Such a person is in continuous remembrance and continually conscious; his consciousness extends this world into the other. Therefore he will be alive eternally.

Continuous remembrance, total consciousness, is the goal and the sign of the perfect human being. It is also the beginning, the means, and the key to perfection.

Perfection is in Allah and is from Allah, and man attains it in the measure of his closeness to Allah.

To come close to Allah is only possible through loving Him, and to love Him is only possible through remembering Him. The Beloved of Allah, Muhammad (may Allah's peace be upon him), said:

man ahabba shay'un akthara dhikruhu

Man remembers often the one whom he loves.

Frequent remembrance of Allah increases His love in one's heart. If one's heart and mind are preoccupied with other things, one will forget the Creator and Sustainer of that heart and will neither remember nor love Him.

It is impossible to realize the Creator only with one's senses and one's mind. It is not easy to submit to Him through reason. But if one remembers Him often, that remembrance will penetrate into one's being—into every part, every cell, deep into one's essence, making one able to remember Him without effort, like a heartbeat. Then the effort to be conscious will be replaced by the pleasure of consciousness. That pleasure will bring the love of Allah. Allah says:

wadhkuru Llahi kathiran la'allakum tuflihun

Remember Allah often so that you will find deliverance from heedlessness, and find happiness.

(Juma', 62:10)

alladhina yadhkuruna Llaha qiyaman wa qu'udan wa 'ala junubihim

Those who remember Allah standing and sitting and lying on their sides. . . .

(Al-i-'Imran, 3:9)

are the heedful men who see the signs of the creation of the heavens and the earth and know that they were not created in vain.

Realization of this is the reward of remembrance. The pleasure of seeing the harmony in the creation, the love felt for the Maker of this creation, are the signs that Allah has opened the eye of one's heart and the gates of His Paradise.

There are only two rewards which Allah bestows upon a human being that He never takes back. One is the pleasure given in the remembrance of Him; the other is the lifting of dark veils from the eye of the heart, so that wherever one looks one sees the Truth in the beauty and power of the Creator. Allah gives wealth and takes it back, fame and takes it back, progeny and takes them back, and life and takes it back. Yet the gifts of His love and truth are eternal.

The opening of the eye of the heart is the opening of the gates of heaven, the promise of Paradise. His Prophet (may Allah's peace be upon him) said, "Upon the gates of Paradise is written the declaration of Allah's remembrance: *la ilaha illa Llah*." (There is nothing but Allah.) He also said, "Whoever wishes to be with me in the green pastures of Paradise, let him remember Allah often."

* * *

Allah encompasses the whole universe. The universe from one end to the other and from top to bottom is similar to the perfect human being, whose nature is in harmony with the Divine nature and whose character is in accordance with Allah's prescribed morals.

The human being is the macrocosm, and the universe is the microcosm. What is above has influence upon what is under it. This is true with the suns and the planets in heaven and with the organs within the physical body of the human being.

It is also true among men that the power of the higher being keeps the lower one under its command. It is as if a man of higher intelligence and ability uses his influence to create a new man out of a weak person.

The closer one is to the perfect human being, the more one will receive. So in the order of the heavens, the heavenly bodies with their sizes and closeness to each other, with energies received from one another, evolve and develop; and as the heavenly bodies evolve and change, the universal order changes. As some celestial bodies disappear, new suns are born. As some planets shrink, others grow larger. Allah takes with one hand and gives with the other.

Allah says:

wa li-Llahi ma fis-samawati wa ma fil-ardi wa kana Llahu bi-kulli shay'in muhita.

And to Allah belongs whatever is in the heavens and

whatever is in the earth (whatever is above and whatever is under, all that is in the realm of the seen and the unseen comes from Him and goes back to Him). And Allah ever encompasses all things.

(Nisa', 4:126)

There are two aspects to everything. One is the manifestation of Allah's beauty and grace; the other is the manifestation of His might and wrath. These are the two hands of Allah.

When Allah wills to bring His beloved servants to their level of potential perfection, He shows them His manifestation of grace and beauty. His servant, covered by the manifestation of beauty within and around him, acts accordingly.

If someone is shown the might and wrath of Allah, he closes his eyes in fear and awe, does not participate, and declines to act.

Remembering Allah is to open one's eyes to Allah's beauty and grace, thus receiving His blessings and, acting upon them, to reach perfection. Forgetting Allah is blindness, hiding oneself from His wrath.

To realize these two sides of everything is the basic understanding of the One Who Encompasses All Things.

In every atom of the whole universe two opposites are hidden; the grace and the wrath, the positive and negative attributes of the Creator, are manifest in everything.

So it is in the moral life of man. The ones who sin do so because they see beauty in sin and hardship in good deeds. The ones who do good deeds see beauty in good deeds and ugliness in sin. When Allah wills to raise you to the level of perfection, He will show you the causes of perfection as beautiful and the causes of the failure of perfection as ugly.

CHAPTER X

The Prophet Jesus Christ
(upon him be peace)

The prophet Jesus, may Allah bless his soul, is always alive in spirit, but his blessed body is dead and gone. His spirituality certainly exceeds his physical existence, for his spirit is from Allah. Since spirit is contained within the body and the body disappears at death, the ones who think that physical being is in the image of the soul and that the two are inseparable, claim that he did not die.

Everything that is created dies. The soul of Jesus (upon him be peace), which is from Allah, is alive, for it is eternal. When the soul rises from the body at death, the coarse matter of the body is left behind. The body indeed is a materialized reflection of the soul, but its form and shape are related to and in harmony with the realm of appearances of this world and will stay in it when the soul leaves it.

The ones who believe that Allah raised Jesus to heaven body and soul say that Jesus (upon him be peace) will return to this world and will live the life of a man, will have family and children. But Allah raised his soul to Him.

As his enemies planned to destroy him, Allah planned to save him.

wa makaru wa makara Llahu wa-Llahu khayrul-makirin.

idh qala Llahu ya 'Isa inni mutawafika wa rafi'uka ilayya sa mutahiruka min alladhina kafaru.

And (the Jews) planned and Allah also planned and Allah is the best of planners. (And Allah saved him from the cross.)
    When Allah said, "O Jesus, I will take you and raise you in My presence and save you from those who disbelieve. . . .

(Al-i-'Imran, 3:54-54)

His being was raised in a spiritual ascension cleansed of the natural elements of this world. Allah says:

wa qawlihim inna qatalnal-masiha 'Isa-bna Maryama rasula Llahi wa ma qataluhu wa ma salabuhu wa-lakin shubbiha lahum.

And for their saying, "We have killed the Messiah Jesus, son of Mary, the Messenger of Allah," and they killed him not, nor did they cause his death on the cross, but he was made to appear to them as such.

(Nisa', 4:57)

He was saved from the cross and lived his natural life amongst his people, and his physical being died a natural death. As Allah quotes him,

wa kuntu 'alayhim shahidan ma dumtu fihim fa-lamma tawaffaytani kunta antal-raqibi 'alayhim.

I was a witness of them as long as I was among them.

But when You did cause me to die, You were the watcher over them.

(Ma'idah, 5:17)

In reality his return is a moral and spiritual one.

They say that his coming will be close to the apocalypse. Some of the signs of the coming of the end are:

* that the sun will rise from the west;
* that there will be an invasion of the Yellow People;
* Gog and Magog will appear;
* Dabbat al-Ard, a miraculous creature, and Mahdi, will appear;
* Dajjal, the Antichrist, will come to rule the world, and Jesus, in his second coming, will slay him.

All these signs are here now and always were. So is the spiritual and moral presence of Jesus, combating Dajjal.

Dajjals are the people of all times whose lives are consecrated to being worldbound. They are the tyrants who have reached high stations, arrogant ones claiming to be owners and rulers of others. Dajjal is the manifestation of the false reality of this world. He is blind in the right eye—thus, he cannot see the truth. Allah says:

The ones who are blind to the truth in this world will not see their Lord in the Hereafter.

Jesus (upon him be peace) is the manifestation of the truth. His combat with the Dajjal is the fight between worldly rationalization and wisdom, the battle between truth and falsehood.

Dabbat al-Ard is a miraculous creature who holds in one hand the staff of Moses (upon him be peace) and in the other the seal of Solomon (upon him be peace), who is to touch with his staff the ones who have submitted to Allah as lambs submit to the shepherd, herding them to Paradise, and who is to brand the faithless with the seal of Solomon, marking them for Hell.

In reality he is the symbol of conscience, which blames the ego for its wrongdoings. In the one hand of conscience, the staff of Moses leads to the inspired state of obedience to the Lord and salvation; while in the other hand, the seal of Solomon is the condemnation of those who are slaves to their egos.

The appearance of Bani Asfar, the Yellow People, is the domination of man by his animal nature.

Gog and Magog appear when falsehood, crime, immorality, heedlessness, shamelessness, and madness appear as normal and preferable things.

The rising of the sun from the west is the dominance of the flesh over the soul.

The appearance of Mahdi, the last imam, is the realization of what Allah says:

wa nafakhtu fihi min ruhi

I have breathed into man from My own spirit.

(Hijr, 15:29)

This is the growth of the seed of Muhammad (may Allah's peace and blessings be upon him) in the perfect human being. The seed will grow into the causal mind, the all-encompassing mercy, and the Divine essence.

The created universe is unique, has its distinct type and character, and is made up only of its own kind. That is how it was when created; that is how it is now; and that is how it will be. That is why it is not related to time, as time is an indication of change. It is accepted that eternity does not have time, but neither is the temporal universe connected to time.

Therefore, there is no sense in asking when will be the end of the worlds. Christians expected it to be in 1000 AD. The Muslims expected it to be between 700 and 800 Hijrah. If thousands of years are added, what is expected is not going to happen, for it has already happened at the beginning and is happening now.

Know that the end of the worlds is a blessed state, a state in which attributes disappear and the essence appears. If you think that for each and every one of us the end of the world comes when the soul leaves the body, you are correct, for that is when your person—with its particular nature, characters, signs, its particular needs and wants—will die, and your soul will remain.

The metaphor of the assembly of body and the soul together on the Day of Resurrection is the gathering and returning of souls to their origin, to their Lord.

Hadrat Muhyiddin ibn al-'Arabi (may Allah sanctify his secret) said:

> Allah has created the universe as the body and made man as its soul. When the perfect human being passes away is when the end of the world will come.

The Prophet (may Allah's peace and blessings be upon him) said:

> As long as there is a human being in this world who says "Allah," the end of the world will not come.

Hadrat Ibn 'Arabi (may Allah sanctify his secret) said:

> As Allah placed the soul in man, He placed man in the universe. As Allah placed the word in man as his purpose, He placed man in the universe as its purpose.

The universe lasts as long as man is in it. The universe without man loses its purpose. And when the essence of man returns to its source, the heavens fold; the stars scatter; the suns darken; the mountains walk; the worlds shatter.

* * *

wa Llahu lahu ul-haqqi wa huwa yahdis-sabil.
Hasbuna Llahu wahdahu wa ni'mal-wakil.
Wa salli 'ala sayyidina Muhammadin wa alihi wa sahbihi ajma'in
wal-hamdu li-Llahi rabb il-'alamin.

Truth belongs to Allah; it is He who shows the way.
Allah, alone, suffices us, and what a fine guardian is He!
Blessings upon our Master Muhammad
and his family and Companions altogether,
and praise is due to Allah, Lord of the Worlds.

* * *

Classic Sufi literature available from Threshold:

Rumi:
Open Secret, Versions of Rumi $9
Translated by John Moyne, Coleman Barks
Unseen Rain, Quatrains $9
Translated by John Moyne, Coleman Barks
This Longing, Poetry & Letters $9
Translated by Coleman Barks, John Moyne
Feeling The Shoulder of the Lion, Poetry & Teaching Stories $9
Translated by Coleman Barks
Rumi: Daylight, A Daybook of Spiritual Guidance $19
Translated by Camille & Kabir Helminski
Love is a Stranger, Selected Lyric Poetry $9
Translated by Kabir Edmund Helminski

Other Sufi Poetry:
The Drop That Became The Sea, Yunus Emre $8
Translated by Kabir Helminski, Refik Algan
Happiness Without Death, Assad Ali $9
Translated by Helminski, Shihabi
Doorkeeper of the Heart, Versions of Rabi'a $8
Versions by Charles Upton

Other Books on Sufism:
The Most Beautiful Names $11
Shaikh Tosun Bayrak
Love is the Wine, Talks of a Sufi Master $9
Shaikh Muzaffer Ozak
What the Seeker Needs, Writings of Ibn 'Arabi $10
Translated by Bayrak & Harris
Awakened Dreams, Raji's Journeys with the Mirror Dede $13
Ahmet Hilmi, translated by Algan & C. Helminski
Inspirations on the Path of Blame $13
Shaikh Badruddin of Simawna, Translated by Bayrak

Send payment plus $3 for 1st book, $.50 each additional to:
Threshold Books, RD 4, Box 600, Putney, VT 05346
Order by phone (credit cards accepted): (802) 257-2779